Elevate
The Art of Lifting Your Life

Donna Tramonte Dougherty

7710-T Cherry Park Dr, Ste 224
Houston, TX 77095
(713) 766-4271

ISBN:

Contents

1

Introduction

A Contagious Message

In 1929, Louis Armstrong recorded the song When You're Smiling. As I listened to it, I began to reflect on the power of a smile.

Our bodies are wired to respond to emotions. When pleasant external forces—such as a scent, a sound, a touch, or a beautiful image—stimulate us, they trigger positive physical expressions. Gratification becomes visible on our faces.

For some of us, smiles come more easily—perhaps we have strong "smiling genes." I come from a family of smilers. My grandmother, mother, and sister smiled more than most people. You'll find us smiling in a crowd, in the car, in the grocery store line, in church, or at the gym.

I always thought smiling frequently was normal—until I became an adult. Strangers would often comment on how much I smiled. So, I started paying attention. Sure enough, I smiled often, but when I looked around, I realized most people did not.

Since smiles are usually a response to pleasant conditions, you might wonder if I live in the real world. I do. I see pain and suffering, and my heart grieves over it. But I believe God has given us the ability to choose where we focus our attention. In a world filled with hurt, we can still find reasons to smile by counting our blessings. We all have them.

Another beautiful thing about a smile is that it uplifts others without intruding on their personal space. A smile can travel; it is persuasive and contagious. It demands acknowledgment—whether by a return smile or an intentional effort to look away. Either way, a simple smile challenges another person with a moment of positivity.

I believe God designed the smile to be shared. It:

• Costs nothing,

• Crosses all cultural barriers,

• Is safe for all ages, and

• Is remarkably easy to use.

Share your beautiful, God-given expression today!

Hot or Cold

You may be familiar with Alice in Wonderland. Alice, a proper young girl, travels down a rabbit hole and enters a strange and unknown land. While in Wonderland, she speaks with the Cheshire Cat.

Alice asks, "Would you tell me, please, which way I ought to go from here?"

The cat responds, "That depends a good deal on where you want to get to."

Alice replies, "I don't know where..."

To which the cat says, "Then it doesn't matter which way you go."

When I read the cat's words, I was reminded of God's statement to the church of Laodicea in Revelation 3:16:

"So because you are lukewarm—neither hot nor cold—I am about to spit you out of my mouth!"

The choices we make and the direction we take matter. It is essential to head somewhere.

God wanted the Laodiceans to make an honest decision about their faith in Him. He identified as hot those whose commitment to Jesus was genuine, fiery, and consuming. He recognized as cold those who openly professed their unbelief. But His strongest warning was to the lukewarm—the self-deluded, the indifferent, and the spiritually complacent. He could not stomach their apathy.

To drive His point home, God used an analogy the Laodiceans would understand. Just six miles north, the city of Hierapolis was famous for its hot springs, which had powerful medicinal qualities. The nearby town of Colossae was known for its cold, pure waters. But Laodicea's water supply was mineral-laden and lukewarm—putrid and only useful as an emetic to induce vomiting.

As the embodiment of life, breath, movement, and growth, the Lord called the Laodicean church to move beyond their spiritually mediocre existence. He knew that a commitment—either hot or cold—would lead them somewhere.

Am I saying that being spiritually cold is better than remaining lukewarm? No. God is saying that. However, this does not mean that a life without faith is ideal. God desires all of us to be intentional about Him. But if that's not where we are, at least choosing to be cold defines our position. And God can work with that. It will lead somewhere.

Not knowing where she was going, Alice asked the Cheshire Cat for directions. In this context, I believe the cat's response was entirely appropriate—he did not make the decision for her. Alice's journey, like ours, would be shaped by her own choice.

How do we know which way to go?

Like the cat said, "That depends a good deal on where you want to get to."

"Elijah went before the people and said, 'How long will you waver between two opinions? If the LORD is God, follow him; but if Baal is God, follow him.'" —1 Kings 18:21 NIV

"But when he asks, he must believe and not doubt, because he who doubts is like a wave of the sea, blown and tossed by the wind."

—James 1:6 NIV

Memory of Divine Significance

Certain events in our lives stay with us. Moments of trauma, surprise, or profound experience seem to hold a timeless—and sometimes divine—significance. Creative thinker Edward de Bono once said, "A memory is what is left when something happens and does not completely unhappen."

At seventeen, I visited a university campus with a friend. While she attended her classes, I wandered the beautiful grounds and explored the halls. At one point, I called for an elevator on the second floor of one of the buildings. The doors opened, and I stepped inside, pressing the button for the first floor. When nothing happened, I noticed an out-of-order sign and turned toward the stairwell—where I was met with providence.

At the top of the stairs, a young man in his twenties sat in a wheelchair. It was clear he had limited use of his arms and legs. A tube and oxygen tank attached to his chair suggested a respiratory condition as well. He greeted me with a smile, taking quick breaths from the tube. Between puffs, he explained that the elevator was often broken, and as usual, he was waiting for his friends to carry him—and his chair—down the stairs.

I had some time, so I stopped to chat. It's the least I can do, I thought. The poor man must have such a miserable life. Honestly, I couldn't imagine living like that. If I were in his position, I thought, I'd rather not live at all.

If words had hands, his next statement would have slapped me.

Unaware of my thoughts, he said, "Every time the elevator breaks, my friends carry me down the stairs in my chair." He took another breath. "I'm always afraid they'll drop me, and I don't want to die."

Inside my head, I yelled, What?! He wants to live?

His words seemed to echo through the halls and back to me again and again. I listened as he continued speaking, struggling to reconcile the spirit and optimism I heard with the physical limitations I saw.

After a while, we parted ways, and I wandered outside. Challenged by what he had said, I sat beneath a tree for the remainder of the day—growing up.

I realized how judgmental and narrow-minded I had been, assuming someone's intrinsic worth or capacity to contribute. In just ten minutes, this man had become an invaluable teacher, profoundly educating me and reshaping my perspective on life.

More than forty years have passed since that visit. I no longer remember the name of the university or even the friend who invited me. But I vividly remember the remarkable man who changed my heart.

That brief conversation—poignant, unexpected, and fateful—was truly a meeting of divine significance... that never unhappened.

"In his heart a man plans his course, but the Lord determines his steps."

—Proverbs 16:9 NIV

Just Like Him

If I had followed in my father's footsteps, I would have become a plumbing contractor. But my dad discouraged it. He wisely recognized the contrast between the raw realities of his job and my developing aptitudes. Forging metal pipes or carrying a bathtub up a flight of stairs on his back was nothing unusual for him. Meanwhile, I rode horses, danced, and wrote poetry.

Over time, I understood his reservations. I realized it wasn't my dad's occupation I wanted to emulate—it was his character.

I watched how Dad cared for others. Strangers quickly adopted him into their families, relying on him for guidance, input, and support in difficult times. When Dad was around, people just felt better.

Author Maya Angelou once wrote, "I've learned that people will forget what you said, people will forget what you did, but people will never forget how you made them feel."

The most significant aspect of our relationships is not simply the good works we do for others, though those are important. What truly matters is our belief in them—the way we affirm their worth and potential. My dad understood this. We are all created for a unique and matchless destiny, and knowing someone believes in us is profoundly compelling.

Jesus was the ultimate master at this. Think about the radical transformation in Mary Magdalene's life. Consider the disciples—fishermen, tax collectors, and ordinary men—whom Jesus empowered so deeply that even after His physical presence was gone, they went on to revolutionize the world.

Following in His footsteps, the apostle Paul wrote these words to the Corinthians:

"I have the highest confidence in you, and I take great pride in you. You have greatly encouraged me and made me happy despite all our troubles." —2 Corinthians 7:4 NLT

By caring about and believing in others, we validate their worth. It is this kind of love that captures hearts.

The apostle Paul learned this from Jesus—because he sought to be just like Him!

"Put on your new nature and be renewed as you learn to know your Creator and become like him."

—Colossians 3:10 NLT

It's About Who We Are

I recently did an internet search on the life of Adolf Hitler. What I read inspired this writing.

We are all aware of Hitler's twisted policies of territorial conquest and racial subjugation. Under his command, approximately ten million innocent people were mercilessly massacred. He murdered human beings without the restraint of conscience—yet paradoxically upheld a lesser principle against eating meat because he opposed the slaughter of animals. The same man who went out of his way to protect animals executed entire families in his death camps.

Hitler claimed to be a Christian, a believer, and a follower of the Lord Jesus Christ. How incomprehensible that he failed to see the disparity between his horrific actions and the upright character of the Christ he professed as Lord. There must be continuity between what we believe and how we live—otherwise, our belief system is flawed.

The Bible is clear on this matter:

"To the pure, all things are pure, but to those who are corrupted and do not believe, nothing is pure. In fact, both their minds and consciences are corrupted. They claim to know God, but by their actions, they deny him. They are detestable, disobedient, and unfit for doing anything good." —Titus 1:15-16 NIV

Humankind is fully capable of professing Christ while committing dreadful acts. But Jesus is searching for authentic followers—not perfect people, but those who earnestly strive to live according to His will. What we claim is irrelevant; it's about who we are. It is the pure in heart who will see God.

While our stories may never make history books, our lives are read by people every day. May they witness a faithful testimony—one etched onto the pages of our hearts, reflecting our sincere attempts to portray the true character of the One we claim to follow.

"You are our epistle written in our hearts, known and read by all men."

—2 Corinthians 3:2 NKJV

"Blessed are the pure in heart, for they shall see God."

—Matthew 5:8 NKJV

"Jesus called out to them, 'Come, follow me, and I will show you how to fish for people!'"

—Matthew 4:19 NLT

Real People, God's World-Changers

Our family recently watched The Nativity, a film about one of the most pivotal events in history. The way the movie portrayed Mary, the mother of Jesus, intrigued me—she rarely smiled. As the woman chosen to bring the Savior into the world, Mary was a world-changer, so I had certain expectations.

In the film, Mary is depicted as a responsible young woman living under Roman rule. King Herod, the ruling authority, was deeply threatened by rumors of another king emerging in the land. His paranoia drove him to ruthless measures, imposing treacherous and often lethal assaults on the common people in an attempt to eliminate any threat to his monarchy.

As I watched Herod's desperate efforts to maintain power, I began to understand the reason for Mary's somber demeanor. Roman soldiers frequently swept into towns without warning, intimidating, capturing, or even killing indiscriminately. Public abuse and brutal punishments were a grim reality of the time. The horrifying sight of human corpses hanging from trees or scaffolding was not uncommon, leaving an indelible emotional toll. In light of this, the film portrayed Mary as someone who had to navigate her emotions and cope with the harsh realities of her day—just like anyone else.

Given Mary's divine calling, I had expected a different portrayal. I imagined a Mary untouched by the world's ugliness, glowing with joy, as if she lived under a constant God-beam. With every on-screen appearance, I searched her face for a hint of happiness. And then, I had a revelation—the film's depiction was actually more accurate.

The movie highlighted the contrast between human frailty and the supernatural power of God. For Jesus to be born both God and man, a human vessel was required. Mary was the perfect representation of humankind—an ordinary young woman living in a broken world, grieved by its sin, deeply aware of its suffering, yet humbly waiting for the arrival of the promised Savior.

God overshadowed a willing and honorable vessel to bring forth the perfect union of flesh and Spirit. Mary did not live an advantaged life, shielded by divine protection. She was not royalty, nor did she possess extraordinary powers. She was simply real—and she was willing.

God is still looking for real people to fulfill His extraordinary purposes. They are the ones who will say, as Mary did, "May it be to me as You have said." From such surrendered hearts, the world continues to be changed.

[1]"I am the Lord's servant," Mary answered. "May it be to me as you have said." Then the angel left her.

—Luke 1:38 NIV

Some Things Are Final—or "Oops"

While lying at the foot of the bed, my dog, Maggie, sat up twice in response to an unusual sound from the kitchen. I had a stomachache, so I ignored her—something I later regretted.

Earlier that day, I had placed three eggs on the stove to boil and left the kitchen to rest. Unfortunately, I forgot about them.

Some time later, Maggie cried to go outside. We had barely stepped into the front yard when I heard a strange noise inside the house.

Rushing back in, I quickly realized what had happened. The water had boiled out of the pan, and the eggs had exploded—hurling their shells and insides onto the stove, cabinets, floor, under the table, and even onto the ceiling. As I opened windows to clear the smoke, Maggie seized the opportunity to snack on the scattered remains.

As I cleaned up, I thought of the childhood rhyme about another famously shattered egg—Humpty Dumpty.

"Humpty Dumpty sat on a wall, Humpty Dumpty had a great fall.

And all the king's horses and all the king's men couldn't put Humpty Dumpty together again!"

Spraying bits of my Humpty Dumpty with Windex and sweeping his remains into the trash, I reflected on how final the end of a matter can be. Humpty Dumpty fell to his doom by foolishly perching his fragile, globular self on a high wall. My eggs had simmered too long under heat and pressure. In such extremes, disaster is inevitable.

The nursery rhyme makes a striking point—even the resources of kings could not undo the consequences of a poor choice. The same is true for us. If we want different outcomes, we must make better choices. Thankfully, God's Word is here to guide us:

• Be self-controlled and alert (1 Peter 5:8).

• Live a godly life (2 Peter 3:11).

• Settle matters quickly (Matthew 5:25).

• Walk in the truth (3 John 1:4).

• Forgive (Colossians 3:13).

• Esteem wisdom (Proverbs 4:8).

• Seek understanding (Proverbs 2:1-3).

• Be humble (Ephesians 4:2).

• Persevere in trials (James 1:12).

• Love God and our neighbor (Luke 10:27).

• Put aside works of darkness while there is still time (Romans 13:12).

You and I still have time to redirect our choices! There is no need to simmer under pressure or teeter on a dangerously high wall—come on down! God's Word is ready to help, and His wisdom is infinite.

After all, He created the egg!

Hmmm... or was it the chicken?

> *"Therefore, dear brothers and sisters, you have no obligation to do what your sinful nature urges you to do. For if you live by its dictates, you will die. But if through the power of the Spirit, you put to death the deeds of your sinful nature, you will live."*
>
> *—Romans 8:12-13 NLT*

Journey to the Crown

On July 4, 2009, after an eight-year hiatus, hundreds of visitors once again climbed the stairs to the crown of the Statue of Liberty in New York Harbor. Public access to the crown had been restricted for nearly a decade following the September 11, 2001, attacks due to safety concerns, as the narrow, double-helix staircases did not meet emergency evacuation codes.

The 354-step climb to the crown is not for the faint of heart. Certain sections are so confining that visitors have experienced claustrophobia, panic attacks, and heat exhaustion. For those struggling, the winding and constricted stairs offer no option to turn back.

The English poet Francis Quarles once wrote, "He that hath no cross deserves no crown." This challenging ascent into Lady Liberty's crown serves as a profound metaphor for life's journey: the higher the calling, the steeper the climb.

Years ago, I faced a personal struggle with anxiety and depression. Unable to change my circumstances, I felt paralyzed—barely able to function day to day. I was emotionally stuck mid-journey, yet I knew I had to move forward.

Thankfully, the climb is not about speed, strength, privilege, or technique. Step by step, second by second, I dragged myself forward. My progress was slow and clumsy, but by fully trusting God and applying His principles, I was able to ascend—ultimately triumphant.

Lady Liberty stands as a beacon, welcoming the tired, the poor, and the huddled masses yearning to breathe free. Both structurally and symbolically, she calls us all to rise higher. Whatever your struggle, you too can achieve the crown!

"Blessed is the man who perseveres under trial because when he has stood the test, he will receive the crown of life that God promised to those who love him." —James 1:12 NIV

> *"Now there is in store for me the crown of righteousness, which the Lord, the righteous Judge, will award to me on that day—and not only to me, but also to all who have longed for his appearing."*

—2 Timothy 4:8 NIV

Stop the Bleeding

In the book of Genesis, God instructed Jacob to gather his wives, Rachel and Leah, along with their children, and leave his father-in-law's homeland. Laban had treated Jacob unfairly for years, and now God was sending Jacob to the land of Canaan.

As Jacob and his family made their covert departure from Laban's camp, Rachel took her father's household gods. These idols were believed to bring prosperity and protection, so when Laban discovered that both his family and his gods were missing, he pursued them. Unaware that Rachel had stolen them, Jacob boldly challenged Laban to search their belongings.

Laban began his search, but before he entered Rachel's tent, she hid the idols beneath her saddle and sat on it. Persuasively, she lied to her father, claiming it was her time of the month and that she could not stand. Thoughtfully, Laban believed her and left Jacob's camp without his stolen possessions.

Earlier, in a conversation with Jacob before leaving their homeland, Rachel and Leah had spoken bitterly about Laban:

"Do we still have any share in the inheritance of our father's estate? Does he not regard us as foreigners? Not only has he sold us, but he has used up what was paid for us. Surely all the wealth that God took away from our father belongs to us and our children..." —Genesis 31:14-16 NIV

Laban's daughters were deeply hurt and offended by their father's betrayal. They felt cheated out of their inheritance. But rather than surrendering her pain to God, Rachel let her resentment drive her to sin—stealing from her father and deceiving him. Her unresolved hurt predisposed her to justify wrongdoing.

This same pattern plays out in countless relationships today. Whether real or perceived, offenses create a degenerative effect, breeding resentment, deception, and self-justified sin. If left unresolved, pain festers, leading to destructive patterns of behavior. As the saying goes, "Hurting people hurt people."

So, how do we stop the bleeding?

The answer is forgiveness.

You may shake your head in dismay, thinking, "You have no idea what happened to me. How can forgiveness fix this? Why should I forgive? I don't want to let that person off the hook!"

I understand those thoughts firsthand. I've had them myself. They gush freely from a wounded heart. But God established the principle of forgiveness for our sake. He wants us to live free from emotional bondage, unshackled by the poison of bitterness. Forgiveness may not be easy, but it is necessary for us to thrive.

Share your concerns with Jesus and walk the forgiveness journey with Him. He understands.

Jesus chose to forgive those who humiliated Him, tore the flesh from His back, forced a crown of thorns onto His head, drove nails through His hands and feet, and mocked His kingship. He knows what happened to you. He identifies with your pain.

> *"We don't have a priest who is out of touch with our reality. He's been through weakness and testing, experienced it all—all but the sin. So, let's confidently approach him and get what he is ready to give. Take the mercy, accept the help."*

—Hebrews 4:15-16 MSG

Rachel carried her pain into the future, just like the idols she would forever have to hide. I urge you, beloved, do not do the same. Lay it down. Apply forgiveness to your situation. With Jesus' help, you can stop the bleeding.

> *"Do not say, 'I'll pay you back for this wrong!' Wait for the LORD, and he will deliver you."*

—Proverbs 20:22 NIV

"If it is possible, as far as it depends on you, live at peace with everyone. Do not take revenge, my friends, but leave room for God's wrath, for it is written: 'It is mine to avenge; I will repay,' says the Lord. On the contrary: 'If your enemy is hungry, feed him; if he is thirsty, give him something to drink. In doing this, you will heap burning coals on his head.'"

—Romans 12:18-20 NIV

Sticks and Stones

As children, we recited the familiar idiom:

"Sticks and stones may break my bones, but names will never hurt me."

If only we could have remained in that state of wholesome innocence. Back then, our harmless threats were limited to words like "poo-poo head" and "stinky feet"—simple, playful insults from uncontaminated hearts.

But as we grew older, our naiveté was lost. Gossip replaced youthful banter. Lies and slander took the place of childhood name-calling. We learned the painful truth: words can hurt.

As Christians, we are called to submit our hearts, minds, and souls to the Lordship of Jesus Christ. When we walk in close relationship with Him, it becomes easier to guard our tongues from evil and keep our lips from speaking lies:

"Keep your tongue from evil and your lips from speaking lies."

—Psalm 34:13 NIV

We are called to reflect His character by ridding ourselves of anger, rage, malicious behavior, slander, and foul language:

"But now you must rid yourselves of all such things as these: anger, rage, malice, slander, and filthy language from your lips."

—Colossians 3:8 NIV

So why do these sins persist?

According to the Bible, damaging words flow from the condition of the heart.

*"The good man brings good things out of the good stored up in his heart,
and the evil man brings evil things out of the evil stored up in his heart.
For out of the overflow of his heart his mouth speaks."*

—Luke 6:45 NIV

Slander has become a significant issue—even within the church.
Author John Armstrong writes,

"While Christians currently debate a host of ethical issues that are very
important to the life and well-being of the church, I fear that too few
of us are willing to actually address a sin that destroys the work of the
Spirit as fast, if not faster, than almost any other sin. I refer to the sin of
slander."

Indeed, wounds caused by sticks and stones are more easily treated
than the deep injuries inflicted by a reckless tongue. Whether spoken
in prayer, whispered in conversation, or publicly declared, slander
damages reputations and crushes spirits.

We must do better. May God teach us and show us mercy. May we put
aside sticks, stones, and name-calling.

As Christians, we can do better.

*"If anyone considers himself religious and yet does not keep a tight rein on
his tongue, he deceives himself and his religion is worthless."*

—James 1:26 NIV

*"If we confess our sins, he is faithful and just and will forgive us our sins
and purify us from all unrighteousness."*

—1 John 1:9 NIV

2

Community

Can Be Better

I recently celebrated my birthday, which brought back memories of a conversation I once had with my mother about my entrance into the world.

She described my grandmother's joyful reaction when she heard that my name would be Donna. My little Italian grandma loved the name because of its Italian origin. She waved her arms in excitement and joyfully skirted around her kitchen.

My mother also told me that on the day I was born, my grandfather stood outside the hospital nursery and danced. One of the nurses, puzzled by his exuberance, asked my mom if she knew who the funny little man at the window was. It was my grandpa, beaming with love for his new baby granddaughter, rejoicing over my arrival into the world.

Wow. What a marvelous foundation of love and celebration I was given to build my life upon.

As I reflect on my gratitude for such a warm welcome, my thoughts drift to the many children who enter the world under far different circumstances. I think of those who are not received with love—those who are abandoned, discarded, or born into homes filled with violence, neglect, or war. My heart would shatter if I could not lift my eyes to God in prayer, confident that He holds each of their lives in His loving hands.

We cannot solve every injustice. But we have been given the remarkable privilege of prayer—and prayers do affect change. Beyond that, we can carry the hope of Christ to others by stepping into righteous causes and acts of kindness.

Has God called you out of your comfort zone? Has He nudged your heart to feed the hungry, serve the poor, comfort widows, spend time with orphans, or care for the sick and elderly? Has He placed a burden on your heart to pray for someone?

While not everything begins with joy and celebration, with our willingness and God's help, the end of any matter can be better than its beginning.

> *"The end of a matter is better than its beginning..."*

> —*Ecclesiastes 7:8a NIV*

> *"The effectual fervent prayer of a righteous man availeth much."*

> —*James 5:16b KJV*

Draw Near

When our son was 18, he performed in a school drama, portraying a young man living on the street—deprived of family and home. His character did not speak a single word throughout the entire play. Instead, from his position in the corner of the stage, he silently watched as a theatrical Jesus multiplied loaves and fish, raised the dead, forgave sin, died on the cross, and rose from the grave.

The most interesting part of his performance was that he wasn't even a drama club member that year. The drama coach wrote him into the script just thirty minutes before the curtain call. It was fascinating to watch his unrehearsed character evolve.

From his lonely spot in the corner, his character was drawn to the scene unfolding before him. He watched, captivated by the love he saw among Jesus and His followers. At first, he observed from a distance. Then, with growing curiosity, he inched closer. Finally, his interest transformed him—from an onlooker to a participant.

As I watched the drama unfold, I wondered how many of us, regardless of status, feel like outcasts. We may live boldly in the sight of others, yet deep inside, parts of us remain quietly huddled in corners, yearning for acceptance.

God created people with an innate longing for companionship and belonging. If isolation had been His intention, He would have created one immortal man in the Garden of Eden. But He declared, "It is not good for man to be alone" (Genesis 2:18). Thoughtfully and purposefully, He formed a world of kindred souls—designed for relationship.

If you find yourself standing on the outside, looking in, there is still time to be written into the script.

Look center stage at Jesus' compelling message of love.

Then—draw near.

Dream Team

You may have heard the name Rico Petrocelli. A retired shortstop for the Boston Red Sox, Rico played a pivotal role in the legendary 1967 Dream Team. Because of his participation in that historic event, he was given a platform to speak to audiences in his later years—one of which was our church.

Rico shared stories from the early days of his baseball career, including his conversion to Christianity. Then, he delivered a powerful message about the moral decay in America over the last forty years. He spoke with striking clarity about an ongoing societal war.

We are all familiar with America's war on drugs and the war against terrorism. But Rico spoke of another war—a battle often ignored or underestimated.

He exposed the deliberate tactics of the pornographic industry, which relentlessly stalks unsuspecting youth and imprudent adults. He warned of how misguided individuals abuse media, internet-enabled devices, and other high-tech tools to provide easy access to indecent content and unsafe associations. These once-innocent advancements have become weapons in the hands of the immoral—targeting individuals of all ages and backgrounds.

At the close of Rico's message, our senior pastor stood to dismiss the crowd. As I sat there, my mind drifted back to something he had shared months earlier about his upbringing in Lebanon.

He spoke of days when gunfire made it too dangerous to leave home for food, of bombs striking nearby apartment buildings, and of friends being forcibly taken from their homes—never to return. The country of Lebanon has been frequently ravaged by war, and he had lived through the horror of it.

I have never experienced war firsthand, but I have known the distress of combat.

As an adult, I was diagnosed with post-traumatic stress disorder. Over the years, a series of betrayals and heartbreaks frayed my emotions to the point of illness. Mine was a different kind of war. There are seasons in life when we are battered by hard times—attacks that come in various forms, sometimes covertly, catching us unaware.

So how do we fight against the influences that undermine our society, our country, and our personal well-being?

Rico emphasized the need to remain alert—to recognize the threats around us. He charged us to be proactive in pursuing what is good, true, and in the best interests of ourselves and others. Most importantly, he urged us to embrace the matchless power of God through Jesus—the only one who can transform hearts and nations.

Believing in God is not a religious event. It is a personal choice that launches a new chapter in life with the One who loves you most.

You can experience the same transformation as Rico. Invite God into your life, and step onto His Dream Team.

"For the LORD your God is the one who goes with you to fight for you against your enemies to give you victory."

—Deuteronomy 20:4 NIV

Look Beyond the Jacket

How often have we misjudged people by assessing them solely based on what we see on the outside?

Writer Baltasar Gracián once said, "Things do not pass for what they are, but for what they seem. Most things are judged by their jackets."

How true this is. We often evaluate people using a superficial, eyeballing standard of judgment—measuring them against a narrow list of external criteria. Then, without considering the depth of their character, their experiences, or their hearts, we mindlessly slap an invisible label on them and carelessly move on.

It's shameful how systematically we do this, forgetting that every person is a whole being—body, soul, and spirit. How much richness and substance remain unheard and unappreciated when we settle for what people seem rather than who they are!

Sometimes, however, something exceptional forces us to take a second look.

The world did just that with Susan Boyle.

Susan was a 47-year-old Scottish woman who dreamed of becoming a professional singer. She auditioned for Britain's Got Talent, and her performance video quickly became a global sensation, viewed over 40 million times on YouTube alone. I watched it a dozen times myself—with tears in my eyes.

Susan was unassuming, her appearance and mannerisms slightly peculiar. She was not glamorous, trendy, or outwardly polished—the kind of contestant easily dismissed. It was clear the judges and audience held low expectations, silently scorning her before she even opened her mouth.

Then came Susan's moment.

She began to sing "I Dreamed a Dream" from Les Misérables, and the very first note sent the auditorium into an eruption of cheers. Her humble presence and magnificent voice carried a message of undeniable beauty and grace.

Susan's voice opened the door for people to truly see her. She was so much more than she appeared!

The Bible warns against this kind of prejudice in James 2:

> *"...If a man enters your church wearing an expensive suit, and another person wearing rags comes in right after him, and you say to the man in the suit, 'Sit here, sir; this is the best seat in the house!' and either ignore the impoverished person or say, 'Better sit here in the back row,' haven't you segregated God's children and proved that you are judges who can't be trusted?"*

—James 2:2-4 MSG

I believe God fulfilled Susan Boyle's dream to get our attention. He expects us to love and value all people equally—not just those who fit our preconceived expectations.

He wants us to look beyond the jackets of those we meet.

He desires that all would have the opportunity to sing!

> *"The goal of this command is love, which comes from a pure heart and a good conscience and a sincere faith."*

—1 Timothy 1:5 NIV

Loving My Neighbor

On a late-night business flight home, I gazed out the window at the bright pockets of civilization twinkling below and whispered to God, "Who are those people, and are they okay?"

I wondered if they were happy. Were they living in turmoil, or had they found peace? At that very moment, how many were smiling, and how many were crying? Who had just been born, and who would soon take their last breath?

The frosty chill from the window hit my face as I pressed against it. Was it cold down there too?

How often do we think about the stranger?

We rush into elevators, turning our backs without a single greeting. We use intimidation on the roadways to get where we want to go. We grow impatient in checkout lines—how dare the woman ahead of us take extra time digging for small change!

Martin Luther King, Jr. once said,

"An individual has not started living until he can rise above the narrow confines of his individualistic concerns to the broader concerns of all humanity."

The Bible simplifies it even further:

"For the entire law is fulfilled in keeping this one command: 'Love your neighbor as yourself.'"

—Galatians 5:14 NIV

I believe the human soul is lacking until we choose to love people outside of our known and familiar circles.

But how do we do that? And who is my neighbor?

Jesus answered this question with a story:

"A man was going down from Jerusalem to Jericho when he was attacked by robbers. They stripped him of his clothes, beat him, and went away, leaving him half dead.

A priest happened to be going down the same road, and when he saw the man, he passed by on the other side.

So too, a Levite, when he came to the place and saw him, passed by on the other side.

But a Samaritan, as he traveled, came where the man was; and when he saw him, he took pity on him.

He went to him and bandaged his wounds, pouring on oil and wine. Then he put the man on his own donkey, brought him to an inn, and took care of him.

The next day he took out two denarii and gave them to the innkeeper. 'Look after him,' he said, 'and when I return, I will reimburse you for any extra expense you may have.'

(Jesus asked) "Which of these three do you think was a neighbor to the man who fell into the hands of robbers?"

The expert in the law replied, 'The one who had mercy on him.'

Jesus told him, 'Go and do likewise.'"

—Luke 10:29-37 NIV

So, who is my neighbor?

My neighbor is the person who lives and looks different from me. The one who holds unconventional opinions and makes choices that differ from mine.

My neighbor is the stranger in the elevator, the driver who takes my parking spot, the woman searching for small change at the checkout line.

My neighbor was born with a unique purpose—a divine promise to impact the world. And for me to see her, consider her needs, and value her contribution—is love.

> *"For the entire law is fulfilled in keeping this one command: 'Love your neighbor as yourself.'"*

—Galatians 5:14 NIV

Luke 10:29-37 NIV (The Parable of the Good Samaritan)

More Than Soup

During a five-day bout with the flu, I made my slow journey from the bed to the couch when my phone rang. A friend was calling to tell me she was on my front porch.

When I opened the door, she greeted me with a large container of homemade chicken soup. She had heard I was sick and made it to help me heal.

As I took hold of the warm container, I had to force back the tears of gratitude pressing against the back of my eyes. I knew my friend's circumstances—her hectic schedule, ongoing health struggles, and financial difficulties. I understood the true value of her gesture, and I was stunned by her thoughtfulness.

She rushed off to work, leaving me once again in the quiet solitude of my condition. I expected to drag myself through the rest of the day, exhausted and achy—but that wasn't the case.

Though my body was still weak, my spirit had been lifted.

Because of her kindness, I felt better.

She had brought me more than soup.

"A cheerful look brings joy to the heart; good news makes for good health."

—*Proverbs 15:30 NLT*

No Small Thing

Ithank God for the thread of hope woven into my life through my relationship with Him.

The last several years have been severe. I almost gave in to self-pity.

Although my struggles are real, they pale in comparison to the suffering of others. In all honesty, I understand that life is not about me. God sees our plight, and He cares about every hair on our heads. Yet, His concern extends beyond our individual troubles—He is working toward a greater, eternal purpose.

As a deep feeler, I cannot ignore the suffering of humanity. Before I understood the power of prayer, my sensitivity felt like a burden, even a handicap. But now, releasing the desperate needs of others to the One who has both the desire and power to rescue has become my duty, my privilege, and my comfort.

Within eight months of this writing, the U.S. experienced 24 separate weather and climate disasters, claiming 253 lives—the highest number recorded. There were nearly 4,000 murders and 500 mass shootings. Conflict-related deaths worldwide are higher than at any other point this century.

Wars and natural disasters have taken thousands of lives, leaving many impoverished, in ill health, or separated from loved ones. And looming over these crises is the lingering fear of a pandemic that has fueled a permacrisis—a world in perpetual distress.

Each year in the U.S. alone, nearly a million children are victimized, and 1,500 to 2,000 die from physical abuse. Globally, women and children are kidnapped or sold for exploitation. Across centuries, the moral fiber of humankind has decayed to such a degree that sex trafficking has become a gainful business.

These realities are disheartening—but if we refuse to face them, our society ceases to function.

Human rights advocate Gary Haugen said,

"God has a plan to help bring justice to the world—and His plan is us."

We often look away from these horrors because they are painful to acknowledge. But as citizens of God's kingdom and occupants of this earth, we must uphold the truth. The convictions, passions, and love God has placed within us exist for a reason.

What are we doing with them?

By shifting our focus beyond our own struggles, we can firmly grasp the thread of perpetual hope that God weaves through our lives. At the end of the day, we will have spent more time praying, acting, and caring about God's purposes than our own.

I almost gave way to self-pity, but God reminded me to think beyond myself!

May we all vow to reach well beyond ourselves.

The outcome promises to be no small thing.

> *"Rescue those being led away to death; hold back those staggering toward slaughter. If you say, 'But we knew nothing about this,' does not he who weighs the heart perceive it? Does not he who guards your life know it? Will he not repay each person according to what he has done?"*

—Proverbs 24:11-12 NIV

> *"For I was hungry and you gave me something to eat, I was thirsty and you gave me something to drink, I was a stranger and you invited me in, I needed clothes and you clothed me, I was sick and you looked after me, I was in prison and you came to visit me."*

—Matthew 25:35-36 NIV

Designed for Connection

The time we spend in the presence of others is meant to be influential. After all, God created us in His likeness—and since He is a relational God, we are also relational beings.

Whether we are engaged in deep conversation with a close friend or simply overhearing a comment from a stranger in a checkout line, our minds instinctively capture and process what we hear. A trusted pat on the back or the sudden jab of an elbow in a crowded train provokes an immediate response. It is natural for one person to impact another.

Youth minister Doug Fields once said,

"We have souls that thrive in the warmth of kindred spirits...God wired us this way."

God uses the rub between people to communicate matters of relevance. He works through casual human interactions as well as through a divinely inspired plan—one that is otherworldly, powerful, and strategic.

God's primary message concerns His love for people. He relies on a perpetual chain of human influence to convey this passion worldwide.

He could have burned an image of His beating heart in the sky. He could have whispered His love through sound waves carried by the wind.

But instead, God thoughtfully chose to communicate the most vital message in the universe to us, through us.

Somewhere between A.D. 85–95, John the Disciple wrote,

"God showed how much he loved us by sending his one and only Son into the world so that we might have eternal life through him."
—1 John 4:9 NLT

John walked with Jesus. The Bible tells us that he was the disciple who rested his head on Jesus' chest. He heard, firsthand, the rhythm of God's love.

John was there when Jesus' heartbeat—and he was there when it stopped.

His relationship with the Lord compelled him to share God's boundless love.

May we adopt this same sense of duty and purpose.

Because in all our relational endeavors, no communication is more powerful, more relevant, or more necessary.

> *"For God so loved the world that he gave his one and only Son, that whoever believes in him shall not perish but have eternal life."*

—John 3:16 NLT

> *"God showed how much he loved us by sending his one and only Son into the world so that we might have eternal life through him."*

—1 John 4:9 NLT

While We Breathe

On national holidays such as Veterans Day and Memorial Day, I recognize the opportunity to take a break from my usual Monday commitments. If your life is anything like mine, you're busy—and you cherish the gift of time.

That said, it's essential to remember that these days of remembrance came at a high cost. The men and women who served and died in our armed forces deserve our tribute. We honor them by remembering their exceedingly great sacrifice. But we can also honor them in another way—by investing in the people for whom they gave their lives.

While you and I still breathe, we have days, months, or years of opportunity to make a difference. We may not be called to serve in the military, but the people we pass on the street, interact with in our workplace, or sit near at school could all use thoughtful consideration.

A wave. A smile. A hug.

Each simple act carries meaning for the receiver.

We can pay someone's bill, deliver a meal, or offer to pray for those in need.

Author William Paul Young wrote these words, spoken by Jesus, in The Shack:

"If anything matters, then everything matters. Because you are important, everything you do is important. Every time you forgive, the universe changes; every time you reach out and touch a heart or a life, the world changes; with every kindness and service, seen or unseen, My (God's) purposes are accomplished and nothing will be the same again."

During these holidays, we remember the fallen—those who made the ultimate contribution to a better world.

While we breathe, let's contemplate our own.

"Greater love has no one than this: to lay down one's life for one's friends."

—*John 15:13 NIV*

"For you have been called to live in freedom, my brothers and sisters. But don't use your freedom to satisfy your sinful nature. Instead, use your freedom to serve one another in love."

—*Galatians 5:13 NLT*

3

Encouragement

A Minute from Now Can Be Brighter

If you're living your best life and every day feels like Christmas, this message may not be for you.

I'm speaking to those who feel overwhelmed by life's burdens—to the ones who sometimes wonder why they were even born.

Someone once said, "If given the opportunity to view the planet before birth, I would have said, 'No, thank you.'"

For many, life feels like an endless cycle of crises, empty love buckets, and crushing disappointments. The weight of these struggles can make despair feel more real than hope. For some, success is measured not by achievement, but by simply surviving another week. Feeling invalid and unseen, they live on the edge of despair, clinging to the strength to endure the fateful passage of time.

The renowned preacher Charles Spurgeon once admitted,

"I am the subject of depression so fearful that I hope none of you ever get to such extremes of wretchedness as I go to."

This was a man whom God used mightily—preaching to crowds of over 23,000 people, influencing history, and leaving behind teachings that are still widely circulated today. Yet this spiritual giant fought relentless battles with despair throughout much of his adult life.

But Reverend Spurgeon did not surrender to darkness. He persevered in faith and led a remarkable life of purpose.

I, too, have walked through the agony of despair for a significant portion of my life. But it is a testament to God's faithfulness that I no longer live in that place.

The good news is that what was available to Reverend Spurgeon is available to all of us!

This revolutionary certainty is echoed in Galatians 3:26-29, where the apostle Paul declares:

"For you are all children of God through faith in Christ Jesus. And all who have been united with Christ in baptism have put on Christ, like putting on new clothes. There is no longer Jew or Gentile, slave or free, male and female. For you are all one in Christ Jesus. And now that you belong to Christ, you are the true children of Abraham. You are his heirs, and God's promise to Abraham belongs to you."

—Galatians 3:26-29 NLT

No matter where you stand on the dark path of despair, a minute from now can be brighter.

You and I have access to the same God that Charles Spurgeon did. The same principles that carried him from darkness into the light of purpose are just as available to us as they were to him.

Yes, Reverend Spurgeon confessed,

"I am the subject of depression so fearful that I hope none of you ever get to such extremes of wretchedness as I go to."

But he did not stop there. He continued:

"But I always get back again by this—I know that I trust Christ. I have no reliance but in Him, and if He falls, I shall fall with Him. But if He does not, I shall not. Because He lives, I shall live also, and I spring to my legs again and fight with my depressions of spirit and get the victory through it. And so may you do, and so you must ..."

Because He lives, you will live also.

"A little while longer and the world will see Me no more, but you will see Me. Because I live, you will live also."

—John 14:19 NKJV

Burden Light

Someone once told me that allowing oneself to grieve for ten minutes a day can be beneficial—even necessary—when the cares of life become overwhelming.

With so much sadness, injustice, and destruction in the world, things can feel unbearably heavy. So, I drag my burdens before God, surrender to His mercy, and allow my tears to flow.

Recently, in our midweek Bible study, we studied the book of Genesis. As we journeyed through its chapters, I gained a deeper understanding of the physical, spiritual, and emotional damage caused by humanity's fall in the Garden of Eden. The crushing consequences of that first sin still echo in people's lives today.

It is astonishing to consider that Adam and Eve were given dominion over a perfect world—a world where creation flourished in all its glory. But through their disobedience, everything changed. Humanity became subject to death, and the earth itself was set on a course toward deterioration.

History and science have recorded the effects: environmental upheaval, increasing disease, pandemics, famine, and apathy toward human suffering. We still find ourselves shocked by greed, selfish ambition, and senseless violence. Ironically, the more humanity advances, the less virtue it seems to display.

We desperately needed a Savior to help us bear the increasing weight of this broken world.

And thank God—Jesus came.

He was the sacrifice required to turn the tables on our despair. He brought hope. And with that, my tears stop flowing.

Though the human race remains bound to mortality, we are no longer destined for a hopeless fate. Through faith in Jesus and His sacrifice in our place, we are given the promise of a glorious eternity in heaven. And while we remain on earth, He shares our burdens.

So, friend, if you are like me—someone who tends to carry things too heavy for your size—I urge you to look intently at the Savior. He will be with you in every moment of grief.

His yoke is easy.

His burden is light.

Then Jesus said, "Come to me, all of you who are weary and carry heavy burdens, and I will give you rest. Take my yoke upon you. Let me teach you, because I am humble and gentle at heart, and you will find rest for your souls. For my yoke is easy to bear, and the burden I give you is light."

—Matthew 11:28-30 NLT

"Against its will, all creation was subjected to God's curse. But with eager hope, the creation looks forward to the day when it will join God's children in glorious freedom from death and decay."

—Romans 8:20-21 NLT

Forever Friend

My heart ached when I read the email that Doris had died. Tears welled in my eyes as I mourned the loss of a dear friend.

I met Doris when she came to work in our business. She was a tall, stately German woman with a warm smile and an unwavering commitment to everything she did. She carried herself with a childlike joy, embracing people with open arms—as if every new acquaintance was a forever friend. Whenever possible, she delighted in celebrating those around her.

Doris had an arthritic condition, yet as a skilled seamstress and crafter, in her spare time she worked indomitably—her crooked fingers creating beautiful, heartfelt gifts for others. Her generosity and thoughtfulness were inspiring.

Throughout her battle with cancer, she was surrounded by a devoted family and faithful friends. But her greatest source of comfort and strength came from her Savior. Doris's love and trust in Jesus Christ was contagious.

As I processed her passing, I found myself sharing her story with others. Yet, to my dismay, my listeners barely acknowledged my words. Their lack of reaction left me feeling disheartened—until I realized why.

They hadn't known Doris.

No matter how much I reminisced, I couldn't bring them to where I was. Hearing about her wasn't the same as knowing her.

That realization led me to a deeper truth:

The same is true of Jesus.

Just hearing about Him is not enough. His relevance only becomes real through personal knowledge. We must know Him.

While I can no longer introduce you to Doris, I can introduce you to Jesus.

The Bible tells us that He stands at the door of your heart and knocks. If you invite Him in, you will quickly come to know Him. He will become your Savior, Comforter, and Forever Friend.

"Look! I stand at the door and knock. If you hear my voice and open the door, I will come in, and we will share a meal together as friends."

—Revelation 3:20 NLT

"The Lord cares deeply when his loved ones die."

—Psalm 116:15 NLT

Good Guys and Bad Guys

Why do the bad guys seem to win?

It's not just in the movies where villains get away with the goods—we see it in our neighborhoods, cities, country, and world. We witness the dreadful behavior of certain people who prosper despite their wrongdoing, slipping away from well-deserved consequences.

King David wrestled with this very frustration when he wrote:

> *"This is what the wicked are like—always carefree, they increase in wealth. Surely in vain have I kept my heart pure; in vain have I washed my hands in innocence."*

—*Psalm 73:12-13 NIV*

David questioned the obvious. Why bother following the rules?

He struggled with the moral reasoning behind making right choices because, from his perspective, the consequences didn't match the actions. The wicked seemed to enjoy the pleasures of sin—and get away with it.

But then, David had a revelation.

In verses 16-19, he writes:

> *"When I tried to understand all this, it was oppressive to me until I entered the sanctuary of God; then I understood their final destiny. Surely, you place them on slippery ground; you cast them down to ruin. How suddenly are they destroyed, completely swept away by terrors!"*

—*Psalm 73:16-19 NIV*

When David spent intentional time in God's presence, he was exposed to absolute truth. Suddenly, he saw justice in a new light.

The limitations of human perspective faded as he gained divine insight into the heavenly realm—where God sees everything, where He watches, and where He judges.

Be comforted, friend—your obedience and sacrifices are not in vain.

If you ever question whether doing the right thing is worth it, I encourage you to do as David did. Spend quiet time with God.

Let Him reveal to you the short- and long-term rewards of being one of the good guys!

> *"Nothing in all creation is hidden from God's sight. Everything is uncovered and laid bare before the eyes of Him to whom we must give account."*
>
> *—Hebrews 4:13 NIV*

> *"And God raised us up with Christ and seated us with Him in the heavenly realms in Christ Jesus."*
>
> *—Ephesians 2:6 NIV*

Grace Over Self-Deception

R everend Tom Ascol once said,

"Self-deception is an insidious condition. You will never meet a person who knows he is self-deceived. By definition, those ensnared are completely unaware that they are."

Self-deceived people often defy truth and reason. They wield weapons of absurdity and irrationality, yet they believe in their causes as strongly as those grounded in truth.

But when lies are unshackled from the mouths of the unjust...

When truth is trampled by corruption...

When the innocent are assailed and wickedness is endorsed...

When faith becomes pretentious and God is mocked...

Sin abounds—and we grieve.

For God's faithful followers, such senselessness stirs a holy uneasiness. We shake our heads in wonder. We pray. We wait for God's intervention and deliverance. But more than that—we learn.

We look to Jesus and learn of His grace.

The Lord desires that all would be saved, and He is not only thoughtful about it—He is proactive.

Where the law identified sin and demanded punishment, grace entered through Jesus' extraordinary sacrifice on the cross.

Grace is the divine space between where we are now and God's unachieved expectation. It is wholly sustaining, patiently enduring, and always available to those who refuse to cling to vain beliefs or worthless idols.

God's amazing grace intensifies in response to the increase of sin. It liberates, it transforms, and it offers endless opportunities for change.

So, while the self-deceived may promote sin in our circles, families, government, and world, we gather our best intentions and fervent prayers.

We bring our teachable hearts to Jesus.

We go to the One who has given us strength, considered us faithful, and appointed us to His service (1 Timothy 1:12).

We accept His grace—and we believe.

May the grace of our Lord Jesus Christ be with you.

"The law was added so that the trespass might increase. But where sin increased, grace increased all the more, so that, just as sin reigned in death, so also grace might reign through righteousness to bring eternal life through Jesus Christ our Lord."

—Romans 5:20-21 NIV

"Let us then approach the throne of grace with confidence, so that we may receive mercy and find grace to help us in our time of need."

—Hebrews 4:16 NIV

Hope

Years ago, I began blogging to share encouragement, empowerment, and hope. At that time, I chose the tagline:

"Those who believe that happiness comes from sunshine alone have never danced in the rain."

This quote exemplifies the freedom we can experience when we transcend our circumstances and step into the unseen realm of hope.

Hope is a beautiful, buoyant expectation of a positive outcome—even in the midst of a bleak or failing situation. It is meant to provoke and sustain us when we are confronted with the impossible.

But what drives people to be hopeful?

A key to hopefulness is the presence of faith—a stabilizing and directional tool.

Faith points us in the right direction.

Hope gives us the strength to move forward.

Consider the connection between faith and hope in these scriptures:

- "Remember your word to your servant, in which you have made me hope." —Psalm 119:49 ESV (Faith in "God's word to him" gave him hope.)

- "The Lord is my portion, says my soul, therefore I will hope in him." —Lamentations 3:24 ESV (Faith in "the Lord as his portion" gave him hope.)

- "Let us hold fast the confession of our hope without wavering, for he who promised is faithful." —Hebrews 10:23 ESV (Faith in "He who promised" gave him the confidence to continue hoping.)

- "In hope of eternal life, which God, who never lies, promised before the ages began." —Titus 1:2 ESV (Faith in "God who promised" gave him hope of eternal life.)

We all have a place we turn to in times of need.

For me, God's presence is the safest place on earth.

I remember when our family vacationed at the Von Trapp Family Lodge, a breathtaking 2,400-acre mountain resort in Vermont. My husband and I decided to hike down the mountain on one of the many trails. Our 9-year-old daughter, Asheley, eagerly asked to come along.

As we walked, she skipped just ahead of us—until she turned onto a different path and quickly disappeared from view.

Dusk had fallen. The woods were dense and threatening.

We called her name, but dreadful silence answered us.

We ran through the darkening forest, uncertain of which path she had taken. My heart pounded, and panic set in. Even my husband's attempts to stay calm were failing.

Was she lost?

Hurt?

Kidnapped?

Then, amid the rising fear, a scripture came to my mind—a lifeline in the darkness:

"The Lord himself goes before you and will be with you; he will never leave you nor forsake you. Do not be afraid; do not be discouraged." —Deuteronomy 31:8 NIV

I had been reading Deuteronomy for several weeks, and in that moment of despair, God's Word steadied me.

We didn't know where Asheley was.

But the Lord did.

He had gone before us.

We reached the edge of the forest, where the sky opened to an expansive grassy hill. Still, no sign of Asheley.

Where was she?

How had we let this happen?

I repeated the scripture, forcing myself to stay focused on hope.

Then, rounding the vista, we finally saw her—sitting peacefully on a fence at the bottom of the mountain!

We all seek hope in times of need.

I contend that if you reach in God's direction, you will find it.

"And now, Lord, what do I wait for and expect? My hope and expectation are in You."

—Psalm 39:7 AMP

"The LORD himself goes before you and will be with you; he will never leave you nor forsake you. Do not be afraid; do not be discouraged."

—Deuteronomy 31:8 NIV

Keep Swimming

If you've seen the movie Finding Nemo, you're familiar with one of its most memorable characters, a cheerful and forgetful fish named Dory. Throughout her journey, Dory chanted a mantra:

"Just keep swimming, just keep swimming, swimming, swimming."

Her short-term memory loss led to some hilariously funny moments. But in truth, it could have been her downfall—if not for her unwavering determination to keep moving forward.

Dory kept swimming.

After battling a stubborn cold for days, I woke up after yet another restless night and told myself the same thing: "Just keep going."

Sometimes, putting one foot in front of the other is all you've got.

The same is true during seasons of worry or stress. When life weighs heavy, the mind becomes cloudy, creativity is stifled, and physical strength is depleted. Yet again, we keep swimming.

Now, forget that Dory is a cartoon character for a moment. Consider how she overcame the obstacles in her life. At some point, she made a choice—a decision to press on despite her limitations.

She could have accepted the world's belief that only the intelligent, quick-witted, and well-equipped succeed. She could have listened to the voices that told her she would never achieve greatness.

But she didn't.

Instead, Dory remained remarkably optimistic. She persevered.

She chose to make her life count.

A simple internet search will yield countless stories of individuals who, despite overwhelming odds, kept their faith and conquered the impossible. The Bible tells us that faith is belief in what we do not see, and the evidence of that faith is receiving what we have believed.

Yet, some individuals struggle to believe in their purpose. Even Job, a prayerful and holy man, once cried out in despair:

"Why did I not perish at birth, and die as I came from the womb?" — Job 3:11 NIV

Life is flooded with economic, societal, and domestic struggles. We may even, at times, feel like giving up. But if we do, the world will miss us.

Each of us was born with a significant purpose.

Job chose to persevere—and was rewarded by God for his faithfulness. So were countless others.

Thomas Edison once said:

"Our greatest weakness lies in giving up. The most certain way to succeed is always to try just one more time."

We were meant to live lives of meaning.

The book of Proverbs reminds us:

"The godly may trip seven times, but they will get up again."

—Proverbs 24:16 NLT

Never Alone

Our niece gave birth to her second daughter, a beautiful baby girl named Caydence.

But shortly after delivery, we received devastating news—something was desperately wrong.

Little Caydence had been deprived of oxygen due to an extra-long umbilical cord wrapped around her neck.

She was rushed to the nearest medical center and placed on life support. The test results were heartbreaking.

Caydence showed little evidence of brain activity.

She could not breathe on her own.

She was incapable of movement.

She had not cried.

She was blind.

In moments like this, the human mind overflows with desperate questions:

Is God aware of the baby's helpless state?

Does she know she is in distress?

Is she afraid? Is she truly alone?

It would be incomprehensible to think she was as alone as she appeared.

Our family wrestled with despair. But then, pulling ourselves back into the reality of faith, we remembered the truth—

We are never alone.

The Bible overflows with promises of God's unfailing love and faithfulness. He assures us that He will not abandon any of us—at any age, under any circumstances.

The God of the universe, the Creator of life, did not forsake little Caydence. Though her fate was beyond our grasp, the One who loved her most was with her.

He had pledged to comfort, protect, and provide for her temporal and eternal needs.

God allowed breath to fill this beautiful child for a purpose.

And for the precious time Caydence spent with her family, we were given the glorious opportunity to exchange love and human touch with her—moments that were timeless, leaving an indelible Caydence-shaped imprint on our hearts.

Caydence abides with God in heaven now.

She is not alone.

She never was.

She never will be.

"But Jesus said, 'Let the little children come to Me. Do not stop them. The holy nation of heaven is made up of ones like these.'"

—Matthew 19:14 NLV

Raising Them, Growing Us

Having raised our three kids into adulthood, I marvel at the superhuman efforts of my parents.

Growing up, I assumed they knew exactly what they were doing—that parenting came with a built-in manual of wisdom and expertise. But when I became a parent myself, I quickly realized the truth: parenting is a "learn as you go" experience—an education gained on our knees, under fire, and quite often, just in the nick of time.

It's not unusual for a parent to take a militant stand on a child-rearing matter while secretly shuddering at the thought that the decision could be wrong. Fortunately, we are not expected to have all the answers. But we are responsible for putting great faith and effort into doing our best—and living an authentic life before our children.

Author Clarence Buddington Kelland once said,

"My father didn't tell me how to live; he lived and let me watch him do it."

So if your decisions are caring and deliberate, and your example is consistent, your believability will become a contagious influence on your children.

God is a present help in times of need. Trust in His established and eternal principles to give you the wisdom you require.

As parents, our challenge is to live our best life, keep the faith, and remain optimistic while our children navigate their own journey.

- As babies, they won't know what you're doing.

- As pre-teens, they won't want to know what you're doing.

- As teens, they won't care what you're doing.

• But as adults, they will marvel at what you've done!

—*Proverbs 22:6 NIV*

Ready to Live

She sat frozen on the couch—motionless, yet inside, everything was unraveling.

Her mind raced like frenzied traffic, thoughts colliding in a terrifying, hollow rush. She longed to run anywhere yet stayed paralyzed in fear of everywhere.

Her hands tingled. Chills and sweat alternated in waves, triggered by the smallest sound. Her body had become reactionary—her senses heightened, sounds magnified, people complicated. Yet, the silence was stifling, and being alone brought dread.

In moments of overwhelming fear, she would whisper the name—"Jesus."

That one word was her entire prayer.

The woman in this story was me.

For most of my adult life, I struggled with anxiety, depression, and, ultimately, panic attacks. I was in emotional bondage—dying inside but desperate to live.

Everyone has their own version of happiness.

Mine was to fully embrace the life that Jesus died to give me.

I wanted to be unencumbered—to live and love freely, to feel joy and walk with purpose. So even in the darkest times, when fear clouded my vision and I couldn't see beyond my pain, I fumbled my way toward God.

And thankfully, He was there.

The Bible tells us that God dwells in the dark cloud.

Even in our most desperate moments—when fear, sorrow, or uncertainty engulf us—He is with us.

Through the Holy Spirit, God became my ever-present help in trouble. He showed Himself strong in my weakness. He embraced me with a love that radically transformed my spirit, soul, and body.

I still pray the name "Jesus."

But not out of fear.

Because I am no longer the woman on that couch.

One day, I looked up—and God's light had undeniably pierced my dark cloud.

I was thawed.

Calm.

Unafraid.

I was ready to live—to step fully into the life He died to give me.

Run to the Roar

The story of David and Goliath is one of the most inspiring tales in the Bible—a young shepherd boy defeating a fearsome giant with nothing more than a slingshot and a stone.

But what gave David the courage to face such an overwhelming foe? How did he find the strength to triumph?

David achieved what seemed impossible, standing firm amidst the mocking jeers of the crowd. Without support or armor, he didn't just confront the giant—he ran directly toward the battle line to meet him.

According to Scripture, David didn't retreat in fear.

He charged boldly toward the roar.

How often do we do the opposite?

If we're honest, we'd admit that we run from much smaller challenges.

- The stress of a demanding job.

- A disappointing result.

- Mounting responsibilities.

- Financial strain.

- The need to forgive.

We often allow these struggles to grow into towering walls of defeat.

But David's courage came from two things:

1. Preparation.

2. Unwavering trust in God.

As a shepherd, he had already faced lions and bears to protect his flock.

Those experiences—guided by God's hand—strengthened his skills and confidence.

By the time David faced Goliath, he knew his battle belonged to the Lord.

We can learn from David's example.

What weapons are you keeping close?

Are you leaning on the lessons and victories God has already given you?

Instead of avoiding the roars in our lives, we must face them with faith, trusting that God has equipped us for the challenges ahead.

Every battle is an opportunity to grow stronger and more confident in God's power to deliver us.

As David proclaimed:

"The Lord who rescued me from the paw of the lion and the paw of the bear will rescue me from the hand of this Philistine." —1 Samuel 17:37

With that same faith, we too can conquer the giants in our lives—

By running toward the roar.

"And all this assembly shall know that the Lord saves not with sword and spear; for the battle is the Lord's, and He will give you into our hands.

When the Philistine came forward to meet David, David ran quickly toward the battle line to meet the Philistine. David put his hand into his bag, took out a stone, and slung it, striking the Philistine in the forehead. The stone sank in, and he fell face down on the ground."

—1 Samuel 17:47-49 ESV

Suddenly Memories

The longer we live, the more we realize that lasting memories don't require swimming with dolphins or skiing the Himalayas. Not everyone has those opportunities.

But here's the good news—adventure isn't reserved for the extraordinary.

A simple touch of spontaneity can turn an ordinary day into something unforgettable.

No matter what physical or financial limitations may exist, God has given us the ability to experience joy on the planet He so carefully and deliberately designed for us.

Recently, my three adult children and I reminisced about their childhood. As they spoke, it became evident that the memories with the greatest impact weren't the big, expensive trips or highly planned events.

Instead, the moments that captured their hearts were born out of spur-of-the-moment ideas—what I like to call a "Suddenly."

A Suddenly happens when a normal, expected activity is interrupted by something new—creating an unexpected, unforgettable moment!

Our two daughters recalled the day I picked them up from school and, instead of heading home, drove straight to the zoo.

Before leaving the house that afternoon, I had grabbed their play clothes and, upon arrival, announced our change in plans.

It wasn't scheduled. It wasn't premeditated. It was a Suddenly.

Decades later, that one spontaneous zoo trip remains one of their most cherished memories.

Our son recalled a snowy drive home from school. His sisters and a friend were in the car, their chatter growing increasingly loud.

Wanting to get their attention, I opened the sunroof—just as giant snowflakes were falling from the sky.

Cold air and swirling snowflakes rushed inside. The children gasped—then laughed as we caught snowflakes on our faces and tongues. We left the sunroof open for much of the ride, letting the winter wonderland sweep us up in the moment.

That, too, was a Suddenly.

The unexpected had lifted us all to a shared, sweet place.

God delights in our joy.

So, make Him happy—and have some fun on this beautiful earth.

Whether you swim with Flipper, see him at the zoo, ski on snow, or catch it on your tongue, Suddenly memories are yours for the making

"So don't be afraid, little flock. For it gives your Father great happiness to give you the Kingdom."

—Luke 12:32 NLT

The God of Grace

For some, it is not easy to believe in a God who was executed on a cross.

In biblical times, many people rejected Jesus as King or God because they simply did not understand His message. Instead, they saw Him as a blasphemer—a threat to their religious order.

They believed He was more likely a criminal than the Messiah and demanded His crucifixion.

Humankind is accomplished at error.

We fail—and judge another's weakness.

We fear—and judge another's fate.

The religious minds of that day could not accept Jesus because He did not fit their preconceived notions. He professed to be their Messiah, yet He did not establish the earthly kingdom they had expected.

To them, Jesus became an offense.

John 1:17 tells us,

"For the law was given through Moses, but grace and truth came through Jesus Christ."

Jesus was the message of grace to a graceless crowd.

They had only known the law.

So, His sentence and execution were easily justified in their minds.

In an attempt to discredit Him, they weaponized the Scriptures—specifically, Deuteronomy 21:22-23:

"If a man guilty of a capital offense is put to death and his body is hung on a tree, you must not leave his body on the tree overnight. Be sure to bury him that same day because anyone who is hung on a tree is under God's curse."

But this Scripture was not meant to condemn Jesus.

It was written about Him—not as a means of judgment, but as a prophetic declaration of the sacrifice He would make.

Jesus was both fully God and fully man.

And so, He did what humankind could not.

He became accursed—taking on our curse and our sin.

As He writhed on the cross, He wrestled against all the powers of darkness.

The atmosphere must have teemed with spiritual warfare.

And then—

In what was perhaps the most powerful moment in history—

Jesus died.

But the story didn't end there.

Jesus was the God who was crucified on the cross—

But He didn't stay there!

You can believe it!

"Grace to you and peace from God our Father and the Lord Jesus Christ."

—1 Corinthians 1:3

"We believe that we are all saved the same way, by the undeserved grace of the Lord Jesus."

—Acts 15:11 NLT

"For sin shall not (any longer) exert dominion over you, since now you are not under Law (as slaves), but under grace (as subjects of God's favor and mercy)."

—*Romans 6:17 AMP*

Up Where We Belong

The old song Up Where We Belong inspired this story.

One spring, a bird built a nest under the roof of our front porch, where she laid her eggs. Soon, two tiny hatchlings were born. We listened to their soft chirps and watched as they stretched their necks toward Mama whenever she returned with food.

They seemed like a happy little bird family.

Then one day, as I passed the porch door, something caught my eye.

One of the babies had fallen several feet onto the concrete floor below. He was barely moving.

I rushed to tell my husband, who went outside and gently lifted the tiny, fuzz-covered creature back into the nest. We wondered if Baby—as we named him—had any hope of survival after such a fall. We also feared that his mother might reject him now that he had been touched by human hands.

But that evening, we saw Mama bird once again perched over both babies.

The bird emergency seemed to be over.

The next morning, I hesitated before looking out onto the porch.

Sure enough—Baby had fallen again.

This time, we wondered if Mama had intentionally pushed him from the nest. Was something wrong with him? Would he ever fly?

I felt terrible for the little guy. We couldn't abandon him to predators, so once again, we lifted him back into the nest.

Three days later, we heard a new kind of commotion on the porch.

Mama and Papa bird were present, fluttering excitedly around the nest. Inside, both babies were chirping and straining their little necks to watch.

They were alert, curious, and strong.

Hurray! Baby was meant to live!

Jesus once said:

> *"Look at the birds of the air; they do not sow, reap, or store away in barns, and yet your heavenly Father feeds them. Are you not much more valuable than they?"*
>
> *—Matthew 6:26*

Birds do not engage in human survival strategies, yet they are still cared for by their Creator.

Jesus wants us to understand and apply this same principle—it is God's provision, not our own ability, that ultimately sustains us.

Baby fell twice from great heights in a short period.

Had someone not been providentially appointed to lift him, he would have died.

People fall as well.

We fall into sin.

We fall from great heights.

When we fall, much is at stake—family, reputation, careers, and relationships. Even when we repent, we may feel hopeless and wonder if there is any way back.

But the Bible reassures us:

"Humble yourselves before the Lord, and He will lift you up." —James 4:10

Just like Baby needed a rescuer, we too need help from someone greater than ourselves.

We need Jesus.

He has been providentially appointed to lift us—

Up where we belong.

"I will exalt you, O LORD, for you lifted me out of the depths and did not let my enemies gloat over me."

—Psalm 30:1 NIV

What Moves You?

We cry for people across the world who suffer the loss of loved ones in tragedies.

We mourn for those who die without knowing Christ—whose cries from an eternal hell cannot be remedied.

Our hearts ache for children whose parents are displaced and for those who must now rebuild their shattered nations.

Even as a child, I felt the weight of human suffering. I often wrote poetry, pouring my emotions onto the pages of a time-worn binder. Looking back through those handwritten verses, I see that injustice deeply shaped my character.

Decades later, tragedy is still a part of life.

But how grateful I am to know Jesus.

Through my faith in Him, I now have access to the throne room of God—a holy and mighty place where His children can lay their burdens and prayers for a hurting world at His feet.

The Bible says:

> *"So let us come boldly to the throne of our gracious God. There we will receive His mercy, and we will find grace to help us when we need it most."*

> *—Hebrews 4:16 NLT*

What moves you?

What burdens arrest your heart?

Like the words in my childhood binder, there are things in this world that shape us.

Your God-given inclinations may be bottled up.

Pop the top.

Let the tears flow.

Pour yourself out at the feet of your God.

Because He longs to be gracious to you.

"Yet the Lord longs to be gracious to you; He rises to show you compassion. For the Lord is a God of justice. Blessed are all who wait for Him."

—Isaiah 30:18 NLT

"In the same way, let your light shine before men, that they may see your good deeds and praise your Father in heaven."

—Matthew 5:16 NIV

What You Cannot See

Sometimes, even our most sincere prayers and best efforts yield no visible results.

We are left confused, asking the question:

"Why?"

This question is especially relevant for women because of their birthing nature.

Women have an intrinsic desire to bring forth new life—whether in childbirth, relationships, creative endeavors, or spiritual callings.

When women labor over something, they expect a particular result—like a baby after nine months of pregnancy.

So, when an effort fails to produce what was intended, the question arises:

"If there is no birth, was the labor in vain?"

Let's consider the birthing process.

Birth begins with conception—

An idea,

A calling,

Something brand new that becomes.

Yet, in the early stages, new life remains unseen. It exists in a place hidden from the naked eye, growing and forming until the time of delivery.

But what if we never see the fruit of our labor?

What does it mean to carry a burden for something never revealed?

I was pregnant four times, but I carried only three children to full term. My second child was miscarried.

Yet, I do not believe for a moment that the conception and early growth of that child were in vain.

In His infinite wisdom, God chose to count her among the inhabitants of heaven—and while I cannot see her, He can.

Job's Children: A Different Perspective

Remember Job?

In the first chapter of his story, Job lost everything, including his ten children.

But in Job 42:10, we read:

"The Lord made him prosperous again and gave him twice as much as he had before."

God restored everything to Job in double measure.

- Before his loss, Job had 7,000 sheep, 3,000 camels, and 500 yokes of oxen.

- After his restoration, Job had 14,000 sheep, 6,000 camels, and 1,000 yokes of oxen.

But what about his children?

In verse 13, we see that God gave Job 10 more children—the same number as before, not twenty.

Why?

Because in God's view, Job's first ten children were not lost.

They still existed somewhere.

Job could not see them—but God could.

This reveals a profound truth:

Not everything that matters is visible.

Choosing to Rest in God's Wisdom

David wrote:

> *"I do not concern myself with great matters or things too wonderful for me. But I have stilled and quieted my soul..."*
>
> —*Psalm 131:1-2 NIV*

Sometimes, no matter how much prayer or effort we pour into a cause, the outcome remains unseen or feels futile.

The challenge is accepting these moments, trusting that they are beyond our control and orchestrated by God for a greater good.

Like David, we can choose to quiet our hearts and release the need to understand everything.

God has given us the ability to trust Him, even when we don't see results.

So carry on.

Your prayers and efforts are not in vain.

Even when you cannot see the result—

What is unseen by you is known by Him.

> *"My heart is not proud, O LORD, my eyes are not haughty; I do not concern myself with great matters or things too wonderful for me. But I have stilled and quieted my soul; like a weaned child with its mother, like a weaned child is my soul within me."*
>
> —*Psalm 131:1-2 NIV*

You Can Always Find Your Way Home

My friend owns three dogs. One day, someone opened their pen—and the fence around her house—and all three ran away.

Two of the dogs, older and more familiar with the neighborhood, were quickly caught by a kind neighbor who saw them running loose. But the youngest, just a puppy, ran away alone.

That evening, my friend laced up her sneakers and walked the streets for four hours searching for her pup.

Regretfully, she thought, "He's so cute—someone probably picked him up."

Heartbroken and exhausted, she finally went home without him.

Then, two days later, she was shocked to find the puppy scratching at her front door.

She wondered, how he found his way home.

He had never been outside the fence before. He had no knowledge of the streets, no experience navigating the unfamiliar world beyond his home.

Then, after reliving her long, winding walk, she realized—

The puppy had followed her scent.

As she shared the story with me, I immediately thought of Jesus.

How attentive are we to the trail that leads us to our Master?

Do we study His map book—the Bible?

Can we detect His presence?

Do we listen for His voice when He whispers to our hearts, "This is the way; walk in it"?

Just as my friend's presence had left a trail for her puppy to follow home, the Lord's presence leads us as well.

No matter how far we stray, no matter how lost we feel—

When we choose to return, we will always find our way home.

"Whether you turn to the right or to the left, your ears will hear a voice behind you, saying, 'This is the way; walk in it.'"

—Isaiah 30:21 NIV

4

Intervention

Daddy's Here

Feeling melancholy, I spent the morning alone, asking God to speak to me.

After a while, I set my computer on my lap to check my email—just in case someone had reached out.

The first email I opened was from a woman at my church.

And inside it was a treasure.

She had sent an image of a Fire Rainbow—a rare and breathtaking phenomenon that had been visible for only an hour along the Idaho border.

The conditions required for such a sight are exceedingly precise.

- The clouds must be cirrus, floating at least 20,000 feet in the air.

- The air must contain just the right amount of ice crystals.

- And the sun must strike the clouds at exactly 58 degrees.

The woman who sent the image had no idea how fascinated I was by such things.

Yet, out of all the people she could have shared it with—she sent the email to only four people.

And I was one of them.

Since childhood, I have been enthralled by the way God paints extraordinary images in the sky to communicate with mankind.

He generously displays His handiwork—evidence of His paternal nearness and certainty.

The Aurora Borealis, more commonly called the Northern Lights, is another stunning example of God's splendor.

He sends them out, and they dance above us—almost as if to say,

"Daddy's here."

At a young age, I believed that such heavenly phenomena confirmed the existence of a loving Creator.

This beauty could not be the product of atmospheric chance—it was fashioned and displayed by divine hands.

Though I may never witness a Fire Rainbow in person, I was overwhelmed by the magnificent image on my lap that day.

When I needed Him most, the God of creation spoke to me—

In a language I would understand.

"Daddy's here."

"She gave this name to the Lord who spoke to her: 'You are the God who sees me,' for she said, 'I have now seen the One who sees me.'"

—Genesis 16:13 NIV

Divine Impact

As part of my practical training in Bible college, I was required to go to a store, purchase items as led by the Holy Spirit, and deliver them to a home of someone I did not know—an address that the Lord would direct me to.

It was early December, and the stores were bustling with holiday shoppers. I prayed for guidance over the excursion, trusting God to lead the way.

After shopping, I knocked on the door of a white farmhouse in town. An older man answered, holding a cellphone to his ear—though he wasn't speaking. He stood just a foot or two inside the doorway, staring at me through the open upper panel of his storm door. There was no barrier between us, yet he seemed hesitant—perhaps intimidated.

I smiled warmly, hoping to put him at ease, and explained the reason for my visit.

"God led me to shop for and deliver gifts to this address."

As I spoke, his eyes widened, and his jaw dropped. Yet he continued to hold the phone to his ear, still not speaking.

From the small bed pressed against the wall behind him, I realized he must live in a one-room studio. This blessed me because one of the gifts we selected was a twin-size heated blanket. We had known buying a size-specific gift was risky, but both my husband and I felt very comfortable with it being the right purchase. Seeing that little bed confirmed—we had stopped at the right home.

I lifted the wrapped package and passed it through the opening in the door. The man reached for it apprehensively, in slow motion—still holding the phone, still not speaking, still staring at me.

I reassured him.

"There are no strings attached to this visit. I'm a Christian, and this is just God's way of blessing you."

Then, I bent down and lifted the second package—a small, decorated Christmas tree.

At that moment, I witnessed the divine impact of my visit. For the first time, the man's eyes left me and locked onto the tree. His entire expression softened.

Then, with excitement, he put down the first package and reached forward, wrapping his arm tightly around the little tree.

In that moment, any lingering hesitation I had about shopping for a stranger burst like a glass Christmas bulb. The heating blanket spoke to me, confirming the right address—but the tree spoke to him. It seemed to be the evidence he needed to believe my words.

As I turned to leave, I smiled and said, "Jesus wants you to know you are loved."

Still holding the phone in one hand and the tree in the other, he beamed—a big, knowing smile.

I hope to revisit him one day. But until then, I will pray for the man with the phone that didn't talk... and the tree that did.

Isaiah 30:21 NIV –

"Whether you turn to the right or to the left, your ears will hear a voice behind you, saying, 'This is the way; walk in it.'"

1 Corinthians 12:4-7, 11 NLT –

"There are different kinds of spiritual gifts, but the same Spirit is the source of them all. There are different kinds of service, but we serve the same Lord. God works in different ways, but it is the same God who does the work in all of us... It is the one and only Spirit who distributes all these gifts. He alone decides which gift each person should have."

Divine Protection

Life is full of close encounters—frightening moments when danger brushes by.

The rush of anxiety spikes, our hearts pound, and then—just as quickly—the moment passes.

We wipe our brows, sigh in relief, and move on as if nothing happened.

Parents, in particular, can relate to the near misses their children experience.

Imagine a baby walker speeding toward the top of a staircase—only to be stopped at the last second by a towel that had fallen from a laundry basket earlier that day.

Had that towel not been there, the outcome could have been tragic.

We all have stories like this.

But what about divinely orchestrated delays?

Could God's angelic response team be behind those unexpected disruptions—

A missed appointment?

A wrong turn off the highway?

An inconvenient delay that saved us from something we never even saw?

The Bible assures us that God cares enough to assign ministering spirits to intervene on our behalf.

Under His command, they divert, catch, answer, comfort, and protect.

They regularly influence our lives in ways we may never realize—preventing disasters and orchestrating blessings.

If even half of these unseen threats had not been averted, our lives would likely look vastly different.

So the next time we experience a divine rescue, let's do more than simply exhale in relief.

Let's take a moment to thank God for His vigilant care and unfailing protection.

—*Psalm 91:11 KJV*

Doesn't Get Better Than That

My grandmother's death did not seem equal to the way she had lived.

Grandma was a sweet, remarkable woman. Born in Italy, she arrived in the U.S. at Ellis Island by boat on December 2, 1912, at the age of twelve. She eventually married, and together with my grandfather, they raised six children through the Great Depression.

Tiny in stature but considerable in character, Grandma had learned to be entirely satisfied with the simple life. She was passionate about people, not things. She loved with organic sincerity and humility, and it was not unusual to see tears in her eyes over a family crisis or tragic news.

Because she was so unique, I expected the moment of her death to be distinctive—perhaps imposing or angelic.

I thought it should be better for her.

Someone as good as Grandma shouldn't just expire like everyone else.

But no symphony played.

No heavenly light shone down.

No grand display marked her departure.

She simply stopped breathing.

And she was gone.

I wrestled with the experience until God graciously put it in perspective.

The lack of a ceremonial display at her death should not define her life.

This life is only relevant for as long as we're here—but eternity is forever.

What truly matters resides on the other side of death.

So, of course, what we see when the soul leaves earth lacks totality.

Grandma died at age 96 of heart failure—the only time I ever saw her ill.

Several days before she passed, she had a spiritual visitation.

She described seeing two women enter her hospital room and mock her.

"You will never see your home again," they jeered.

"You will die here."

She said they ridiculed her repeatedly until a man's voice from outside her door demanded they leave.

She never saw the man.

Frightened, she told the hospital staff what had happened, and they moved her to another room.

When my father called to tell me, I rushed to the hospital.

On the way, I prayed for wisdom.

Before I reached her floor, I felt a strong conviction—Grandma wasn't sure she was going to heaven.

Her life was hanging in the balance between heaven and hell.

No wonder she was afraid.

She was days away from death, and I had the privilege of preparing her for eternity.

I leaned over her frail body and softly asked, "Grandma, do you believe you'll go to heaven when you die?"

With minimal strength, she whispered, "I haven't been good enough."

What a statement!

She had given and given to others—she was a good person!

But in the hours before death, when she was closest to meeting her Creator, she was confronted by unworthiness.

I took her hand and said, "Oh, Grandma, it's not about that. None of us are good enough. Jesus isn't looking for your goodness—He's looking for your heart! He will forgive your sins and prepare you for heaven!"

That day, I had the honor of sharing God's great love with Grandma.

And she accepted Jesus as her Savior.

She continued having visions until she died.

But after that day, they were no longer frightening.

She spoke of beautiful white horses and friendly faces that brought her comfort.

And then, one night, her heart quietly stopped beating.

She left this world without a sound.

So it's true—her death did not seem equal to the way she lived.

But her eternity will far surpass anything I could have wished for her.

She lives forever in the glorious presence of God, her Heavenly Father.

And it doesn't get better than that.

"Precious in the sight of the LORD is the death of His saints."

—Psalm 116:15 NIV

"Then God will give you a grand entrance into the eternal Kingdom of our Lord and Savior Jesus Christ."

—2 Peter 1:11 NLT

Evidence

God created the Earth as a thoughtful, visible kingdom for our pleasure and habitation. He generously spread evidence of Himself throughout creation to compel us toward Him. May we not take His purposeful gestures for granted.

How often do we disappoint or insult our Creator by gazing upon a sunset, a waterfall, or a blossoming flower without recognizing their divine significance?

God's intricate and sustaining handiwork is a living depiction of His creativity and love.

He has placed us in a world overflowing with beauty—bountiful in things that delight our senses.

We see His great glory in the upholding of time and the endurance of nature. He illustrates His care for us through His attention to detail.

We are warmed by the sun and nourished by the rain. By daylight, we see. By twilight, we rest.

Martin Luther once said, "God writes the gospel not in the Bible alone, but on trees and flowers and clouds and stars."

Yet we often overlook the passionate and graphic evidence of His presence—evidence that dances from rain to sea and seed to plant.

I wonder what the world would be like if God decided to roll up Earth's canvas.

What if He removed the light?

Without wind or rain, how would the planet be clean—how would it smell?

If rivers stilled and vegetation withered, how would we be sustained?

What if there were no more sound—no breaking waves, brushing leaves, or music?

What if God was no longer creative, generous, playful, or loving?

It is difficult to imagine such devastation from One so faithful.

Our God has indeed given us all things to enjoy!

Thank Jesus today for the touch of time, the scent of life, the vista of expectancy, and the sound of heaven.

My friend, taste and see that the Lord is good.

Behold the evidence!

"They know the truth about God because He has made it obvious to them. Forever since the world was created, people have seen the Earth and sky. Through everything God made, they can clearly see His invisible qualities—His eternal power and divine nature. So they have no excuse for not knowing God."

—Romans 1:19-20 NLT

From Panic to Peace: A Dance in God's Garden

Life is not all sunshine and rainbows. We live in a world where problems are part of life, and some days the weight of our cares overwhelms us. We become disheartened and long to refresh our senses with beauty, truth, and hope.

One day, I received devastating news, and within seconds, my body was engulfed in anxiety.

I knew from experience that if I didn't release the stress quickly, it would be harder to overcome.

A wave of panic washed over me from head to toe.

"No," the word leaped from my mouth. "God, please don't let the panic attacks return!"

And then—amid the storm—I felt a small burst of clarity.

I was not without resources.

The Lord promises He will never leave us—ever.

I prayed for help to release the stress.

The raging sensations didn't subside right away, but as I compelled my mind to pray, clarity began to take hold.

And in that moment—God filled my mind with a garden of words.

Join me in this garden, where our faithful Creator unshackled my mind and renewed my spirit.

As we wrestle with unbelief for a better day, we stumble upon a garden of hope.

In this garden, an array of flowers surrounds us with incomparable beauty and an elevating bouquet.

We feel the soft brush of virgin growth and sense the fresh purity of life as the flora around us wave upward toward their Maker.

The atmosphere tugs at our hearts and beckons us to participate.

Compelled, we acknowledge the wonder.

We remove our shoes and dance among trusted companions.

In this garden, we enjoy the freedom to dig into rich soil.

Here, we unearth treasures of truth.

In this garden, we find the confidence to plant ourselves into the substance of God's will.

Here, we join with those who reach toward the heavens; we worship the Son and wait for the appointed time when He will send us a quenching rain.

The Bible tells us to "Be joyful in hope."

In this garden, it is easy to do.

"And this hope will not lead to disappointment. For we know how dearly God loves us because He has given us the Holy Spirit to fill our hearts with His love."

—Romans 5:5 NLT

More Than Coincidence

Albert Einstein once said that a coincidence is God's way of remaining anonymous. Even this esteemed brainiac recognized that certain events in our world defy science, law, and reason—clear evidence of God's handiwork.

Throughout my years as a Christian, I have stood in awe of God's considerate and deliberate dealings with humankind.

His purposeful intervention in people's lives and His tenacious work to fulfill His will on earth cannot be ignored.

Nothing God does is haphazard.

So when our physical and non-physical worlds align in uncanny ways, we can be certain it is divine design!

There is a story in this book, Place in This World, about our granddaughter Bella, who was adopted by our oldest daughter and her husband.

I'm excited to share an event that occurred in Bella's early days with us.

Our daughter-in-law, Michelle, mentioned that she had been searching for a black baby doll as a gift for Julianna, Bella's new four-year-old sister.

Since Bella is African American and her new family members are Caucasian, Michelle felt that a baby doll resembling Bella would be a sweet and thoughtful gift.

She had searched in several local stores but had yet to find the right doll.

As she shared her frustration, I suddenly remembered a black baby doll that I had owned over 40 years ago!

I rushed to retrieve her from storage.

The doll had a beautiful face, just like Bella, with dark curly hair. However, her outfit had become threadbare over the decades, and she needed a good scrub.

I planned to give the doll to Michelle so she could fix her up as a gift for Julianna.

But Michelle insisted that since the doll had once been mine, I should be the one to pass her along.

As I dressed the doll in a new outfit, I happened to notice the embossed branding on her plastic back.

What I read took my breath away.

I blinked. Looked again.

There it was—clear as day. The name "Bella" was imprinted on the doll's body!

In quotes.

I smiled big and thought,

"What a coincidence!"

"But the plans of the LORD stand firm forever, the purposes of His heart through all generations."

—Psalm 33:11 NIV

Place in This World

God, the ultimate Father, is attentive to every child's life path.

Some children are born into families, while others are born for families.

Bella Rose was born for ours!

When she was just two days old, our four-and-a-half-year-old granddaughter held her new baby sister in her arms for the first time.

Bella had been born across the country to a woman who could not care for her.

In selfless love, her birth mother chose adoption, and our daughter and son-in-law were chosen to be her forever family.

The call came at 4:00 p.m. on a Monday.

By 4:00 a.m. Tuesday morning, they were on a plane.

Just a week and a half later, with the paperwork complete, their family of four flew home!

When God calls something into being, the details can fall into place quickly.

We could not have chosen a more perfect child for our family or orchestrated a smoother transition.

Even though God is grand and imposing, He delights personally in the purpose and placement of a tiny child's life.

He is amazing!

"For You created my inmost being; You knit me together in my mother's womb. I praise You because I am fearfully and wonderfully made; Your works are wonderful; I know that full well. My frame was not hidden

from You when I was made in the secret place. When I was woven together in the depths of the earth, Your eyes saw my unformed body. All the days ordained for me were written in Your book before one of them came to be."

—Psalm 139:13-16 NIV

God knows us before we are born.

He is deeply and passionately aware of who we are and where we belong.

"The Lord gave me this message: 'I knew you before I formed you in your mother's womb. Before you were born, I set you apart and appointed you as My prophet to the nations.'"

—Jeremiah 1:4-5 NLT

"But even before I was born, God chose me and called me by His marvelous grace. Then it pleased Him to reveal His Son to me so that I would proclaim the Good News about Jesus to the Gentiles..."

—Galatians 1:15-16a NLT

Before Bella was ever born, God knew her.

He had already defined her place in this world.

She was born for a purpose.

She was born for our family.

"God sets the solitary in families."

—Psalm 68:6a NKJV

Relationship with God

I recently read this scripture:

—*John 8:31-32 NASB*

I paused to contemplate the amazing truth available to us when we read the Word of God.

Who wouldn't want to be enlightened by knowing the truth about something significant to them?

Who doesn't need help to face or manage the sting of life's realities?

Who hasn't searched for clarity amidst confusion or freedom from a haunting problem?

God's Word offers spiritual enlightenment that leads to a freer and fuller life.

Beyond just reading, our connection to God deepens when we spend time alone with Him.

"Draw near to God, and He will draw near to you."

—James 4:8a NASB

The more we are with Him, the more we know Him.

I prefer reading the Bible at night because I am not a morning person.

However, I wanted to demonstrate my seriousness about growing in my relationship with God.

So, for several months, I set my alarm for 5:00 a.m., grabbed my coffee, my blanket, and my Bible, and headed to the porch.

What I encountered through this simple discipline was transformative!

What Changed?

1. I was drawn to the person of Jesus Christ.

His actions were selfless, uncompromising, and loving.

If justice was needed, He embodied it.

If mercy was required, He expressed it.

His responses weren't dictated by the voices around Him but by absolute truth.

He balanced justice and mercy, majesty and humility, judgment and compassion—because He was both human and divine.

As I read, I became fascinated.

In those early hours, I met the true Jesus—not the one I had been introduced to by others, but a Jesus of exotic tenderness, affection, and compassion—

and I fell in love with Him.

2. Jesus became a trusted companion.

This was significant for someone like me, carrying the scars of betrayal.

As I studied His faithfulness, I began to welcome Him into the secret places of my heart—

unreserved and unafraid.

3. God's words became personal and conversational.

He began to guide me, offering wisdom, comfort, and even caution at times.

I was amazed at how alive and timely His truth was.

As I learned to hear His voice through my eyes on the page, my life was forever changed.

Abraham Lincoln once said:

"I am busily engaged in the study of the Bible. I believe it is God's Word because it finds me where I am."

The words "it finds me where I am" beautifully capture just how personal this journey is.

Consider the Bible, my friend.

Buy the book. Download the app. Start reading.

The format doesn't matter. The starting point doesn't matter.

What matters is that you take time to show God you are serious about your relationship with Him—

and experience your own transformation!

> *"Christ became human flesh and lived among us. We saw His shining greatness. This greatness is given only to a much-loved Son from His Father. He was full of loving-favor and truth."*
>
> *—John 1:14 NLV*

> *"Those who know Your name trust in You, for You, Lord, have never forsaken those who seek You."*
>
> *—Psalm 9:10 NIV*

Something to Hold

I was deeply hurt by someone I had implicitly trusted. It wasn't the first time, and the weight of betrayal left me paralyzed, caught in a mind swirl of confusion and heartbreak. As a result, I became distrustful of almost everyone, anxious, and emotionally drained.

I struggled to overcome the pain, frantically searching for hope. I poured out my heart to God, expressing my longing to touch Him and be held by Him. In my despair, I prayed for something tangible—something to hold onto.

God responded with a gentle whisper: "Hold onto my Word."

At that moment, I made a decision—I would carry my Bible everywhere. It became my constant companion. I took it with me to the grocery store, restaurants, and even to work. Wherever my feet went, my Bible went too.

I read it at every opportunity, drinking in the words like a thirsty sponge.

Over time, God's truth and promises overwhelmed me. His words penetrated the wounds of my heart, slowly releasing the pain and anxiety I had buried so deeply. Through the pages of His book, Jesus became so tangible that He fulfilled my desperate need for contact. I knew without a doubt that the living, present God had touched me.

Thirty years later, He still resides in my heart as an abiding life force, reminding me that He is near, and I am never alone. Through His Word, He has not only healed the trauma of my past but has made me stronger, wiser, and empowered to face an undefined tomorrow.

Though heartbreak may strike again, I am ready.

I know my God is near, and through the loving embrace of His Word, I have been given something to hold onto.

"Every part of Scripture is God-breathed and useful one way or another—showing us truth, exposing our rebellion, correcting our mistakes, training us to live God's way. Through the Word, we are put together and shaped up for the tasks God has for us."

—2 Timothy 3:16-17 MSG

Tackled

Families gathered in the hallway as our Bible study ended, filling the air with indistinct chatter. As I navigated through the crowd, a distinct sound caught my attention.

A young girl spotted her friend and called out her name with such pure joy that I could almost feel the excitement in her voice. It was as if she had found something precious that had been lost. Her spontaneity and affection were so striking that I muttered, almost to myself, "Wow, I wish someone would greet me that way."

Although I spoke casually, my words carried a deeper significance. The book of Luke teaches that what we say reflects the true state of our hearts. That little girl's greeting was genuine, and so was my quiet longing.

It had been less than two weeks since my only sibling and dearest friend, Cheryl, had passed away. Her loss left a hole in my heart the size of a fist. She had battled illness for a long time and had recently been admitted to the hospital with stage four cancer. For over 30 years, whether on her feet or in her sickbed, Cheryl had faithfully served the Lord. At her memorial service, over a thousand people came to honor her. Many sought out family members to share how she had profoundly impacted their lives.

My tears were a mélange of sorrow and hope. Her death stirred untested parts of my soul. I had prayed for countless individuals who had lost loved ones, but now I found myself asking: How do they reconcile such loss? The feeling of unfinished business was intense. There were things I still wanted to say, moments I still wanted to share, and love I still wanted to give.

The family took turns visiting Cheryl at her hospice bedside, waiting for a rare moment when she was strong enough to speak. As she slept, my thoughts wrestled between heartbreak for our family and frustration over her suffering. I prayed endlessly, "Lord, are we really going to lose her?" The idea seemed incomprehensible.

I braided Cheryl's long, wavy hair and stroked her face, wanting nothing more than to hold her close before she left this world. But her fragile body could not withstand a full embrace. Instead, I settled for a gentle kiss on her forehead and a knowing smile.

Back in the church hallway, just seconds after my whispered longing, I was tackled from behind.

I stumbled, regaining my balance, and turned to see a radiant little girl peering up at me. She was about eight years old, African, with lovely braided hair. I didn't know her name, but she had her arms wrapped tightly around my waist.

I looked into her sweet face and whispered, "You heard me?"

I hadn't thought anyone had heard me.

"Thank you for the hug."

She beamed up at me, her smile sparkling with warmth.

In that moment, I knew that God had inspired this child's purposeful actions. Her hug was strong, affectionate, and deeply comforting—uncannily reminiscent of the hug I had longed to give Cheryl.

I stood there, astonished by the thoughtful ways God works in our lives.

Ecclesiastes 11:5 tells us:

> *"As you do not know the path of the wind, or how the spirit comes to the bones in the womb of a pregnant woman, so you cannot understand the work of God, who does all things."*

The little girl ran off to find her friend while I stood still, collecting my thoughts.

I wondered—had God made Cheryl aware of this moment? Had she seen what just happened? Did she understand what it meant?

I'll ask her when I get to heaven... shortly after I tackle her with a big hug.

> *"God blesses those who mourn, for they will be comforted."*
>
> *—Matthew 5:4 NLT*

> *"My thoughts are nothing like your thoughts," says the Lord. "And my ways are far beyond anything you could imagine. For just as the heavens are higher than the earth, so my ways are higher than your ways and my thoughts higher than your thoughts."*
>
> *—Isaiah 55:8-9 NLT*

The Dream and Mom's Alzheimer's

Throughout my life, I have moved many times, but this move was particularly challenging. My mother, suffering from Alzheimer's disease, was living with me, and we were relocating back to our home state where we had family and better healthcare options for her.

To ease the transition, I temporarily moved Mom to her sister's house. Packing and moving were already overwhelming, but for someone with Alzheimer's, the confusion would be unbearable. I had learned this the hard way during a previous move. I would pack, and she would unpack. Together, we would sort items to donate, only for her to circle back and rethink every decision. I knew it was best to leave her with my aunt while I resettled us.

Unfortunately, the buying, selling, and moving process took longer than expected, and in that time, Mom's mental health declined. Usually, she was childlike, playful, and easy to redirect. But when she couldn't remember a word or lost track of what she was doing, she would grow overwhelmed and take her frustration out on my aunt.

Managing Mom's emotional well-being was harder than keeping up with her medications, doctor's visits, and bills. I didn't want to be her mother—I needed one myself. I longed for her to hold me, to assure me that things would get better. But reality was merciless. The days ahead would only grow worse. The mother I needed was being stolen from me by a cruel, relentless disease.

As a teenager, I had a dream about my mother that stayed with me for decades. It was one of those fateful dreams—the kind that wakes you with a pounding heart and a damp pillow.

The dream began in the most ordinary way: Mom stood at the kitchen sink, the warm, familiar image of home. I expected her to turn, smile, and say something pleasant. Instead, she turned slowly, her face eerily vacant, her body still and unanimated. She was present, but somehow, she wasn't there.

Then, something happened that sent a chill through me.

Before my eyes, her long brown hair gradually turned gray—not strand by strand, but in a steady, deliberate wave, like a shadow moving across the sun. The change swept over her, one side to the other, as if time itself was accelerating. She didn't notice it happening. She stood unaware, while I watched in growing horror.

I woke up gasping for air, shaken to my core. The dream had hurled me into a confrontation with the inevitable death of my mother, a reality I was not ready to face.

For years, the dream remained tucked away in my memory, until now.

Fast forward fifty years. The doctor advised me that moving Mom to long-term care should happen immediately. I pushed back, asking if he meant in a few months. He clarified, "I mean very soon. Or right now."

Within weeks, our family made peace with the reality we had been dreading—Mom could no longer stay home. Her memory loss had progressed too far.

Surprisingly, her transition to the nursing home was smoother than expected. With the right care, her playful, childlike self returned. She believed she was on vacation at a beautiful hotel.

During my visits, she would light up with joy, calling my name from across the room. I clung to those moments. But one day, something changed.

She examined my face with a puzzled, almost frightened expression. Then, in a hesitant voice, she asked:

"Are you... Donna?"

I swallowed hard.

"Yes, Mom. It's me."

She was fine after that—but I wasn't.

I walked to my car as I always did, but for the first time, I felt utterly alone. We were losing each other, and nothing I did could stop it.

Looking back, I now understand the dream.

God had given me a glimpse of my mother's future—a warning wrapped in love. He showed me the acceleration of time, the disconnection, the gradual loss of awareness.

Like a father who reads his child a bedtime story, God sat beside me in that dream and whispered the future in a way my heart could bear.

The day Mom passed away, I walked from the nursing home to my car by myself. The same steps I had taken countless times before.

But this time, because of the dream, I knew the truth. I wasn't alone.

Job 33:14-16 TLB

"For God speaks again and again, in dreams, in visions of the night when deep sleep falls on men as they lie on their beds. He opens their ears in times like that and gives them wisdom and instruction."

-John 21:18 GNT

"I am telling you the truth: when you were young, you used to get ready and go anywhere you wanted to; but when you are old, you will stretch out your hands and someone else will tie you up and take you where you don't want to go."

The Helper

Each year, America is grieved by senseless school shootings. One of the most heartbreaking tragedies occurred at Sandy Hook Elementary School in 2012. The loss of 20 young children and six adults at the hands of a 20-year-old gunman devastated the nation.

I work for a ministry that operates a school from daycare through grade eight, and I wondered what we should tell our students about such horrifying news. What message would parents across the nation give to their children?

I came across a timely quote from the late Fred Rogers, creator of Mr. Rogers' Neighborhood. He once said, "When I was a boy and I would see scary things in the news, my mother would say to me, 'Look for the helpers. You will always find people who are helping.'" He went on to say, "To this day, especially in times of disaster, I remember my mother's words, and I am always comforted by realizing that there are still so many helpers—so many caring people in this world."

We thank God for the helpers—the heroes who risked or sacrificed their safety to protect the students that day. People like Dawn Hochsprung, the principal who lunged at the shooter in an attempt to stop him. The teachers who quietly hid and comforted anxious children behind locked doors. The brave first responders, medical personnel, counselors, clergy, and countless others whose vital involvement continued long after the attack.

USA Today quoted one first responder as saying, "The worst tragedy that I've seen... We live in a fallen world where scary things happen." Mrs. Rogers gave her son good advice—look for the helpers. But what if there is no time to find help? What if human intervention is not enough?

The Bible tells us that when Jesus was preparing to return to heaven, he reassured his disciples that they would never be alone. In John 14:16, he said, "And I will ask the Father, and he will give you another Helper to be with you forever." That Helper is the Holy Spirit. He is with us at all times, so we do not have to face the scary things alone.

Saint Augustine once prayed, "O Holy Spirit, descend plentifully into my heart. Enlighten the dark corners of this neglected dwelling and scatter there thy cheerful beams." The Holy Spirit is omnipresent because he is a member of the Trinity; He is God. He can be anywhere and everywhere. He can calm fear, bring peace that surpasses understanding, and hold us in his presence even in our final moments.

I believe that those who lost their lives at Sandy Hook were not alone. They looked for a helper, and the Holy Spirit was there.

So, what do we tell our children? We share a true, powerful, and comforting story.

It begins with Christmas, when God sent Jesus to earth as a baby. Fully God and fully man, Jesus grew up among us, destined to rescue the world from sin. In the greatest display of love ever known, he gave his life on a wooden cross so that anyone who believes in him might have hope and salvation. Then, after Jesus ascended to heaven, the Holy Spirit—the Helper—came to be with us.

So, we tell our children this: Look for the Helper—he will always be there.

John 14:16-17 NCV I will ask the Father, and he will give you another Helper to be with you forever—the Spirit of truth.

5

Reflective

God Sent

As a snowflake flurries down to fall upon the ground,

In hordes of softening, whitening frost, it falls without a sound.

To cover up a world with white through whirling turns in flight,

To paint a picture through the day or secret in the night.

On Christmas morning, I woke up, headed to the kitchen for coffee, and was met with a breathtaking sight—a gentle, unhurried snowfall. The flakes danced gracefully through the air, layering the world in soft white. Being a New England native, the sight of snow on Christmas morning carried me back in time.

I remembered the day I saw the biggest snowflakes ever. It was Christmas Eve, and I was about eight years old. As we left my grandparents' house, the night transformed into something magical. The snowflakes were enormous, floating down from the sky like delicate wafers. To a young girl, it was enchanting—a picture-perfect moment of wonder.

Back in my kitchen, coffee in hand, I smiled at the memory. I was grateful for the nostalgic interlude, a moment of quiet joy that inspired me to write again after more than a year. I have learned to cherish the ability to recall the beauty of past blessings—how they can bring calm to a troubled present.

Our family had been on a tumultuous journey. In my time away from writing, my sister endured her third cancer surgery. My mother and her husband moved back to New England to be with family, and we built an apartment for them in our home. Shortly after moving in, my mother had to have her kidney removed due to cancer. My father suffered a heart attack, stroke, and open-heart surgery, while my husband faced severe physical challenges and broke his neck in an auto accident.

The days of childhood innocence may have passed, but the gifts that fall from heaven have not.

The Bible tells us in Isaiah 55:10-11:

Just as God commands the snow to fall, he speaks life, healing, and purpose over the earth. Even in seasons of hardship, his Word never returns void. His will blankets the world like fresh snow, covering, renewing, and fulfilling its purpose in our lives.

Psalm 107:20 NLT He sent out his word and healed them, snatching them from the door of death.

Guard Your Heart

The scriptures tell us in Proverbs 4:23 to guard our hearts because the wellsprings of life flow out of it. The Message translation of the Bible puts it this way: "Keep vigilant watch over your heart; that's where life starts!"

What do you allow yourself to listen to? What words do you permit into your heart? According to the Bible, words have the power to pierce like an arrow, cut like a sword, and trickle down into our innermost parts. They have access to our insides, where they can latch onto our character, and even our health. That's why we must learn to keep the gateways to our hearts closed to unwelcome traffic.

Our pastor once preached about the many gates leading into ancient Jerusalem. Each gate was strategically constructed and carefully monitored, controlling access to the city's interior. In the same way, we have spiritual and emotional gates leading into our lives. Whether spoken words bring healing or harm, they have equal access if we do not vigilantly guard our gates.

When Nehemiah rebuilt the walls of Jerusalem, he set guards at every gate. These gatekeepers were responsible for monitoring who was allowed in and out, opening and closing the gates accordingly. This illustrates a vital principle—gates offer protection.

There are many things in life that we cannot control. However, what we listen to, where we go, and who we surround ourselves with are within our power to choose. God thoughtfully designed the human body for portability, allowing us to step away from unhealthy influences.

For instance, I've realized that movies have a profound effect on me, so I'm intentional about what I choose to watch. When others say, "I was on the edge of my seat," or "I cried through the whole thing," they're often praising a film's emotional depth. But for me, certain movies can stir emotions that linger long after the screen goes dark. Some impressions are hard to shake, so I've learned to be discerning about what I allow into my heart and mind.

So, be intentional about guarding your heart. Set high standards for what crosses your personal gateways. Like the city of Jerusalem, your heart is worth protecting, because this is where life starts.

Nehemiah 7:2-4 NLT

"I said to them, 'Do not leave the gates open during the hottest part of the day. And even while the gatekeepers are on duty, have them shut and bar the doors. Appoint the residents of Jerusalem to act as guards, everyone on a regular watch. Some

Go to Your Room

Raising three children—two girls and a boy—was an adventure filled with laughter, learning, and, at times, sibling squabbles. Our daughters, less than two years apart, were often at odds, requiring me to step in as a mediator. When all efforts at reconciliation failed, my last resort was to separate them by sending each to her room.

But what happened next always made me smile. Once alone, my two little opponents quickly became the closest of friends. They would crouch on either side of the air vent between their bedrooms, whispering and giggling as if they hadn't just been at war. The moment they were isolated, they instinctively sought a way to reconnect, and the voice of the other became a welcome comfort.

In much the same way, when we step away from the noise and distractions of life, we realize how much we long for connection—not just with people, but with God. When we intentionally separate ourselves from the busyness that keeps us preoccupied, we begin to hear His voice in the quiet.

How often were you sent to your room as a child? And now, as an adult, how often do you go there voluntarily—to sit in quiet conversation with God?

Jesus Himself set this example. He frequently withdrew from the crowds, carving out moments of solitude to be alone with His Father. If the Son of God made time for stillness, how much more do we need it?

Just as my daughters instinctively sought each other once separated, we, too, will find that when we step away and quiet our hearts, the voice we long for most is there—ready to whisper and giggle with us.

Mark 1:35 NLT Before daybreak the next morning, Jesus got up and went out to an isolated place to pray.

James 4:8a NIV Come near to God and he will come near to you...

It Takes Just a Flicker

The sun peeked through the trees, warming my face as I sat on the porch. Something so radiant, beautiful, and powerful must have been created by One even more brilliant, exquisite, and supreme.

God created light for our benefit—both the physical light of the sun and the spiritual light of His Son, Jesus Christ, the Light of the World. Yet how often do we miss His coming? He shines bright and warm, illuminating our path, yet we fail to see, feel, or follow. The world's pervasive darkness is so deceptive that it numbs us. We slip into a spiritual slumber, oblivious to the evil that surrounds us.

Even Jesus' disciples struggled with this. In Mark 8, He warned them to be careful of sin, yet despite walking with God Himself, He pointed out that their eyes failed to see and their ears could not hear. His solution? Remember. Jesus urged them to recall what they had witnessed of Him—to look back at the light they had already seen. Even a flicker of memory has the power to pierce the deepest darkness.

What do you remember of God's goodness? How have you seen His hand in your life?

As I sat on the porch, I reflected on how God has been my warmth in frigid times, my rescue in trials, my strength in weakness. He has been my teacher, my champion, my greatest love. Remember what He has done for you and dispel the darkness.

It takes just a flicker.

John 1:5 NLT The light shines in the darkness, and the darkness can never extinguish it.

Lesson from a Rabbit

As I approached a bend on the back roads to work, traffic suddenly stopped. Curious, I stretched my neck out of the window to see what was causing the delay. In the middle of the road sat a large, indistinct, grayish blob. I assumed it was an injured cat.

Within moments, the driver at the front of the line jumped out and carefully moved the creature to the side. I was surprised when he lifted it. It wasn't a cat at all—it was a giant tortoise! Once the tortoise was safely placed in the brush, the line of traffic resumed. I shook my head, recalling a similar incident from when I was about ten years old.

A friend of mine had two large white rabbits and she asked me to care for them while she was away. We moved their cage into our garage, and I loved the responsibility—though I was occasionally stressed out by their occasional escapes from their cage. Every day after school, I rushed home to tend to my soft, cuddly friends.

One afternoon, however, I opened the garage door and was devastated by what I saw. There, in the middle of the floor, was a large, flat, white figure—completely crushed. Right where my dad's truck had been parked! My heart dropped. Had one of the rabbits escaped and been run over?

Panicked, I slammed the garage door shut and ran into the house, sobbing, "Daddy killed a rabbit!" My mom called my dad to warn him before he got home, then spent the afternoon trying to console me.

When my father arrived, he went straight to the garage. I braced myself for his solemn apology. But instead, he walked in with a bemused expression and said, "Donna, everything is fine. Both rabbits are in the cage. What you saw was a white rag."

Wow. Shocked. Relieved. Embarrassed. In a matter of seconds, my devastation turned into sheepish laughter.

That day in the garage and the day the tortoise stopped traffic, I had been utterly convinced that my perceptions were correct. But I was wrong. What I thought I saw dictated my emotions and actions—yet my conclusions were completely inaccurate -- not true at all.

It makes me wonder: How often have I made the wrong judgment about something truly important? Worse, how often have I misjudged a person? The human mind can be fooled, misled, and utterly convinced of falsehoods. We can be persuaded by incomplete information, personal bias, or even our own fears.

To our consolation, God calls us to live in a dimension that craves, recognizes, and accepts the truth, and he graciously gives us the tools we need to do it.

1. The Bible is filled with wisdom and guidance, offering light when our own understanding falls short.

2. The Holy Spirit walks with us, leading us away from error and toward clarity, discernment, and the purest of reality.

That's the truth.

John 8:32 ERV You will know the truth, and the truth will make you free.

Reciprocal Love

Love is a beautiful thing—something we all long for and cherish. But imagine loving someone deeply, desperately, and unconditionally, only for that love to go unnoticed or unreturned. This is unrequited love—the ache of giving love that is never reciprocated.

In 1 John 4, we read that God is love. He is not just loving—He is the very essence of love itself. Love originates in Him, flows from Him, and is defined by Him. Yet, despite His boundless affection, His gestures are often ignored, overlooked, or rejected.

The Bible tells us that when God created humankind, He said:

> *"Let us make human beings in our image; make them a reflection of our nature..."*

(Genesis 1:26 MSG).

God designed us to reflect His love so that we could experience intimate fellowship with Him. His desire was for us to embrace Him fully, to love Him in return, and to delight in His presence—just as He delights in us. And yet, in the purity of His love, He gave us free will.

He could have assured himself of our life-long devotion. He could have been our addiction, our solitary passion! But true to God's character, he chose instead to give us the freedom to embrace or reject him. The God who is love wants our devotion to him to be heartfelt, not mandated.

God longs for us to respond to His love. He desires moments of tenderness, surrender, and deep connection with us. If we open our hearts, we will find that His love is not just beautiful—it is the most fulfilling, transformative love we could ever know.

Will you return His love today?

1 John 4:16 NLT

"We know how much God loves us, and we have put our trust in his love. God is love, and all who live in love live in God, and God lives in them."

My Prayer

God, indeed, You are my first love. Yet each day, the cares of this world overshadow my worship. Responsibilities snatch me from the secret place where I long to remain with You.

If I had my way in the Spirit, I would stay at Your feet—Your words my food, Your presence my fulfillment. If I had my way in the natural, I would spend every moment speaking to lost people on Your behalf so that they would not miss the great gift of salvation that is freely theirs. I would not turn aside to lesser things. I would not allow earthly turmoil to blind me to the hope that is mine. And I would make it my mission to share that hope.

If my body were able, I would not sleep, but I would spend the quiet hours of the night listening to every whisper You breathe in my direction. Being with You is more enlivening than a night on my pillow.

This world is heavy with burdened hearts. Problems press in. People thrash about in desperation. As we enter a new season, I pray that the compelling witness of the Father, the Son, and the Holy Spirit would shine ever brighter—bringing comfort, deliverance, and salvation to many. Lord, awaken the sleepers, the lovers, the workers, the haters, the weak, and the strong! Shine, Lord—shine brightly!

Mountains and oceans, fruit-bearing trees, blue skies, and rainbows all speak of You—yet so many still wander through life, needlessly lonely and lost. You are too great to be missed! Draw them into the secret place. Awaken their senses!

Open their eyes—let them glimpse the sunbeams through the clouds. Open their ears—let them hear the symphony of Your natural world. Let them feel the touch of the Living God—let the wind of the Holy Spirit brush against their faces. Feed them from the banquet of Your Word!

I pray this in Jesus' name. Amen!

"But he never left them without evidence of himself and his goodness. For instance, he sends you rain and good crops and gives you food and joyful hearts."

—Acts 14:17 NLT

"For ever since the world was created, people have seen the earth and sky. Through everything God made, they can clearly see his invisible qualities—his eternal power and divine nature. So they have no excuse for not knowing God."

—Romans 1:20 NLT

The Better Thing

You may be familiar with the story in Luke 10 about two sisters, Mary and Martha, who were blessed by a visit from Jesus. When Jesus and his disciples arrived, Martha busied herself with serving their guests, while Mary sat at Jesus' feet, listening intently as He spoke. Frustrated by her sister's lack of help, Martha asked Jesus to intervene. But instead of siding with her, Jesus gently pointed out that Mary had chosen the better thing.

Reading this passage, I found myself wondering: Am I more like Martha or Mary? The answer seemed obvious—I am a Martha. Like her, I rush through my days at full speed, tackling endless to-do lists. I bring work home, spend more time managing responsibilities than reading my Bible or praying, and often measure my success by how much I accomplish. Surely, I'm a Martha.

But something prompted me to read the passage again—slowly this time. As I studied the two sisters and their choices, I realized I related to Mary more than I thought. She let her heart guide her. Her love for Jesus overrode the distractions, compelling her to sit with Him and simply listen.

Martha, though well-intentioned, allowed her sense of duty to overshadow the deeper purpose of Jesus' visit. When Jesus comes calling, it is time to turn off the stove, shut down the computer, and focus on the divine. He does not come because he wants food. He is food.

Mary craved time with the Master, giving him her full attention when He arrived. Jesus, the Bread of Life, showed up to satisfy her hunger, not His.

Luke 10:38-42 NIV

*"As Jesus and his disciples were on their way, he came to a village where a woman named Martha opened her home to him. She had a sister called Mary, who sat at the Lord's feet listening to what he said. But Martha was distracted by all the preparations that had to be made. She came to him and asked, 'Lord, don't you care that my sister has left me to do the work by myself? Tell her to help me!'

'Martha, Martha,' the Lord answered, 'you are worried and upset about many things, but few things are needed—or indeed only one. Mary has chosen what is better, and it will not be taken away from her.'"*

Do Not Arouse or Awaken Love Until It So Desires

The Song of Solomon is a captivating portrayal of God's deep affection for His bride—the church. It paints a vivid picture of the sacred romance between God and His people.

"Do not arouse or awaken love until it so desires."

These words are penned multiple times throughout the book, carrying a profound message.

In our walk with the Lord, there are seasons when He calls us to deepen our relationship with Him, drawing us into a sweeping, transformative experience.

In these moments, our spirit rises above our soul, our humanity is laid bare before Him, and we encounter God in a depth of intimacy beyond words. His presence becomes rich with perceptive fullness—so weighty with divine love that all else fades.

It is an experience that is both authentic and sacred.

The passage reads, "Do not arouse or awaken love until it so desires."

When the bride's desire is fully awakened, the Bridegroom comes to meet her.

This divine meeting is yours for the asking.

Pursue God as you would the deepest love of your life. Seek Him. Chase Him. Wait for Him.

And when the time is right—expect to be swept off your feet.

> *"Daughters of Jerusalem, I charge you: Do not arouse or awaken love until it so desires."*

—Song of Solomon 8:4 NIV

The Only You

If I eat something sweet, can you taste it? If rain runs down my face, I can you feel it?

Each of us was born with the ability—and the right—to experience life in a way that no one else ever will. God designed us with an exclusive, deeply personal way of seeing, feeling, and responding to the world. The same sun rises on all of us, the same waves crash against the shore, and yet, how we perceive and process these moments is uniquely our own.

This is not by accident. Our Creator is intentional. When He formed mankind, He made the conscious choice to give each of us our own DNA, an individual fingerprint, and a purpose that can never be duplicated. He could have made us uniform, predictable, or interchangeable—but love does not mass-produce. Love creates.

God delights in the one-of-a-kind masterpiece that is you. The Bible describes Him as the Good Shepherd, willing to leave ninety-nine sheep to go after the one. That's how much He values you—your journey, your gifts, your irreplaceable place in this world.

So, taste the sweetness. Feel the rain. Embrace what stirs your soul and moves your heart. Be fully you. The world doesn't need another copy—it needs the only you.

Luke 15:4 NIV "Suppose one of you has a hundred sheep and loses one of them. Does he not leave the ninety-nine in the open country and go after the lost sheep until he finds it?"

The Value of You

You have a matchless, purpose-driven, divinely appointed place and calling. Without you, the world would be lacking. Right now, in this exact place, your presence matters. The people you have touched, the conversations you have had, and the moments you have influenced would not exist in quite the same way without you.

You are so important that God knew you before you were born. He didn't simply allow you to exist—He intentionally designed you. The Creator of the universe counts the very hairs on your head and has set His unwavering love upon you.

Yes, people will fail you, but Jesus never will. As the embodiment of love, He showers you with affection and faithfulness. The very nature of who He is protects, nurtures, and cherishes you as His beloved.

Today, put aside life's disappointments and rest in the Lord's rightful care for you. Let these scriptures settle deep within your heart. You are chosen, cherished, and called. There is no one else who can fulfill your unique imprint or unrivaled destiny in the world.

Matthew 10:29-31 NIV

"Are not two sparrows sold for a penny? Yet not one of them will fall to the ground apart from the will of your Father. And even the very hairs of your head are all numbered. So don't be afraid; you are worth more than many sparrows."

2 Timothy 1:9 NIV

"...who has saved us and called us to a holy life—not because of anything we have done but because of His own purpose and grace. This grace was given us in Christ Jesus before the beginning of time..."

Through God's Eyes

s I lay my head on my pillow, I noticed an obscure glow outside my bedroom window. From where I lay, I could see the porch jutting out from the back of the house.

Reaching for my eyeglasses, I quickly realized that the glow was coming from the Christmas tree we had set up on the porch the day before. I laid back down, reflecting on the spiritual significance of that moment.

In Psalm 119, the Scripture states, "Open my eyes so I can see what you show me of your miracle-wonders. I'm a stranger in these parts; give me clear directions." With my natural eyes, I could distinguish a blur of illumination, but without definition or clarity. Even when I squinted, I saw only obscurity and vagueness. I knew something was there, but I couldn't fully appreciate the wonder of it—not until I put on my glasses.

When we view life through our natural perspective alone, our vision is limited. We will see hints of beauty, but without God's insight, much remains unclear. Only when we look through His eyes can we truly see the full brilliance of what surrounds us.

Ask the Father to show you what He sees. Peer through the eyes of your Creator, and distinguish the true splendor of your surroundings, the beauty of the people in your life, and the visible expression of God's love that decorates our great earth!

Isaiah 32:3 NIV

"Then the eyes of those who see will no longer be closed, and the ears of those who hear will listen."

Your Story

I purchased an oil painting of a woman in a lovely vintage dress and hung it over my bed. Today, I found myself gazing at her, wondering about her life. Where did she live? Was she a woman of her time, or did she challenge the norms of her era? What was her story?

Evidence from the past often stirs both reflection and curiosity in me. I think about the history of abandoned homes—once filled with life, now standing empty and forgotten. Once places of shelter and community, they have been stripped of purpose, their cold and crumbling frames longing for footsteps to cross their thresholds again.

I wonder about the people who hung the now-faded curtains, who built the red brick stairs, or who once pushed a laughing child on the tire swing that still sways in the breeze. What were their lives like? Did they raise children, have hobbies, or own pets? Did they live in peace or in turmoil? And the greatest question of all—when they left this earth, did they find themselves in heaven or hell? Though they are gone, their lives have left an imprint, a silent echo that speaks to us even today.

> *"The choices we make about the lives we live determine the kinds of legacies we leave."*

— *Tavis Smiley*

What legacy will you leave behind? When your story is told, what will it say? Will the way you overcame pain and faced giants inspire future generations? Will your passions, your joys, and the way you loved others influence those who come after you?

Like prayers that transcend time, our choices today shape tomorrow's world. God designed a universe where every life has meaning, and every decision has lasting impact. Our choices—both great and small—become a bold and timeless testament to what mattered most to us during our time on Earth.

Consider them well—because they tell your story.

Psalm 145:4 NLV

*"Families of this time will praise your works to the families-to-come. They
will tell about your powerful acts."*

Proverbs 3:1-6 TLB

*"My son, never forget the things I've taught you. If you want a long and
satisfying life, closely follow my instructions. Never tire of loyalty and
kindness. Hold these virtues tightly. Write them deep within your heart.
If you want favor with both God and man, and a reputation for good
judgment and common sense, then trust the Lord completely; don't ever
trust yourself. In everything you do, put God first, and he will direct you
and crown your efforts with success."*

Colossians 1:10 TLB

*"And asking that the way you live will always please the Lord and honor
him, so that you will always be doing good, kind things for others, while
all the time you are learning to know God better and better."*

About The Author

DONNA TRAMONTE DOUGHERTY grew up in the quiet beauty of New England, with a tender heart and a feel for grace. From a young age, she wanted to know what life is really about. A sensitive soul, she learned to walk through a world of wonder and pain.

Sorrow and betrayal touched her, but they didn't define her. With the Lord's gentle presence, those hard places became open doors—showing her who she is, why she's here, and the steady, strong power of grace.

Email: dougherty339@gmail.com